Ottawa Ontario Book 1 in Colour Photos, Saving Our History One Photo at a Time

Photography
by Barbara Raué
2016

Series Name:
Cruising Ontario

Book 146: Ottawa Book 1

Cover photo: Parliament Hill, Centre Block, Page 10

Series Name: Cruising Ontario
Saving Our History One Photo at a Time
in colour photos

Books Available in Alphabetical Order:
Aberfoyle, Acton, Alton, Amherstburg, Ancaster, Arthur, Aylmer, Ayr, Bloomingdale, Brantford, Burlington, Caledon, Caledonia, Cambridge, Clifford, Conestogo, Delhi, Dorchester to Aylmer, Drayton, Drumbo, Dundas, Eden Mills, Elmira, Elora, Essex, Fergus, Guelph, Hagersville, Hamilton, Hanover, Harriston, Hespeler, Jarvis, Kingston, Kingsville, Kitchener, Linwood, Listowel, London, Lucknow, Mono, Mount Forest, Neustadt, New Hamburg, Niagara-on-the-Lake, Oakville, Orangeville, Orillia, Owen Sound, Palmerston, Peterborough, Petrolia, Port Elgin, Preston, Rockwood, Sarnia, Seaforth, Sheffield, Shelburne, Simcoe, Southampton, St. Jacobs, St. Marys, St. Thomas, Stoney Creek, Stratford, Thamesford, Tillsonburg, Waterdown, Waterford, Waterloo, Welland, Wellesley, Windsor, Wingham, Woodstock

Book 123-124: Kingsville
Book 125-127: Woodstock
Book 128: Thamesford
Book 129-132: St. Marys
Book 133-136: Sarnia
Book 137: Petrolia
Book 138-139: Welland
Book 140-145: Kingston
Book 146-149: Ottawa

Other Books by Barbara Raue

Coins of Gold

Arrows, Indians and Love

The Life and Times of Barbara
Volume 1: Inventions That Have Enhanced My Life
Volume 2: Entertainment That I Have Enjoyed
Volume 3: East Coast Trips
Volume 4: Olympics Have Always Intrigued Me
Volume 5: Wonders of the World
Volume 6: Caribbean Cruises We Have Enjoyed
Volume 7: Animals
Volume 8: Storms and Other Major Disasters in My Lifetime
Volume 9: Wars, Terrorist Attacks and Major Disasters

The Cromwell Family Book

Laura Secord Discovered

Daddy Where Are You?

Montana Series
Book 1: Montana Dream
Book 2: Life on the Montana Frontier
Book 3: Montana to Boston and Back

Visit Barbara's website to view all of her books
http://barbararaue.ca

Table of Contents

After the union of the two Canadas in 1841, Kingston, Montreal, Toronto and Quebec were in succession the seat of government. During the 1850s these cities contended for designation as the permanent capital of Canada. During Queen Victoria's long reign, the nation of Canada was created, grew and flourished. Queen Victoria ascended the throne in 1837, the same year that violent rebellions broke out in Upper and Lower Canada with demands for a more democratic and responsible form of government. These rebellions prompted many reforms, including the unification of Upper and Lower Canada into the Province of Canada. In 1857, Queen Victoria chose Ottawa as Canada's capital, a political compromise as well as a more secure distance from the American border. In 1867, Queen Victoria signed the *British North America Act* to create the Dominion of Canada, a self-governing nation within the British Empire, established through peaceful accord and negotiation. The Fathers of Confederation reaffirmed the choice and Ottawa as the capital for the new Dominion.

Parliament Hill sits at the heart of Canada's Capital, overlooking a river that reflects many histories. From the beginning, Parliament Hill was designed as a workplace for parliamentarians, and also as a place where everyone could come to meet, talk or just relax in a beautiful outdoor setting. Today there is a scenic promenade which follows the shoreline of the Ottawa River.

The Centre, East and West blocks of the Parliament Buildings were built between 1859 and 1866 (excluding the Tower and Library). The Parliament Buildings have vaulted ceilings, marble floors and dramatic lighting which create an air of dignity. The stone walls have a lot of decoration.

The Centre Block is home to the Senate Chamber (east half), the House of Commons Chamber (west half), and the Library of Parliament. The Hall of Honour stretches through the centre of the building and symbolically links all the elements of the Centre Block together.

The Peace Tower was completed in 1927 and is 92.2 metres tall. The Peace Tower is a campanile, a freestanding bell tower. In addition to the bells that chime every quarter hour, it houses the carillon. The Carillon is a percussion instrument of tower bells played from a large keyboard. The Peace Tower Carillon has 53 bronze bells of different sizes covering 4½ octaves and weighs 66 tonnes.

The carillonneur brings the bells to life by bringing down the large keys with partially closed hands and by depressing the pedals with the feet. Each clapper, pulled by a steel wire, strikes the interior of the bell with just the force given to the key. The performer may then play as expressively as a pianist.

Like the tower itself, the carillon and its music reinforce Canada's dedication to peace. At its inauguration in 1927, Prime Minister Mackenzie King described the carillon as "the voice of a nation in thanksgiving and praise which will sound over land and sea."

On the third floor of the Peace Tower is the Memorial Chamber, a richly carved room of gentle light built to honour Canadians who died in the armed conflicts in which Canada has fought since Confederation.

The Library of Parliament preserves and protects Canada's legislative past. The Library uses the tools of the electronic age to support parliamentarians in their work. The Library offers information, reference and research services to parliamentarians and their staff, parliamentary committees, associations and delegations, and senior Senate and House of Commons officials.

The Library has more than seventeen linear kilometers of materials in its collection including books, periodicals, government documents, CD-ROMs and videos. Parliamentary clients can also tap into on-line databases, an electronic news filtering system, and an on-line catalogue of information right from their desktops.

Canada's Parliament consists of three parts: the Queen (our Head of State) represented by the Governor General; the appointed Senate; and the elected House of Commons. The Governor General calls Parliament together after every general election, reads the Speech from the Throne outlining the government's objectives, and approves all bills passed by the Senate and the House of Commons.

The Senate has 105 members appointed by the Governor General on the advice of the Prime Minister. Senators can serve until the age of 75.

The House of Commons has 308 members elected to represent the people in their ridings. Our Constitution says that a Parliament cannot last longer than five years, after which a general election must be held. Members sit in the House of Commons Chamber which is decorated in green following the tradition of the British House of Commons.

The Constitution authorizes Parliament to make criminal, defence, international trade and broadcasting laws. Senators and Members of Parliament study, debate and often make changes to legislative proposals or bills. Bills are usually proposed by the government and introduced in the House of Commons. The Senate also initiates legislation but any bills to collect or spend public funds must originate in the Commons. Both Houses must approve bills in identical form before they can become law. Bills become law when they receive Royal Assent by the Governor General or a deputy.

A Parliament is made up of one or more sessions. A session can last a few days or several years. It ends when it is prorogued by the Governor General, at the request of the Prime Minister. A Parliament comes to an end when the Prime Minister asks the Governor General to dissolve it and call a general election. The Constitution requires Parliament to meet at least once a year. Usually Parliament sits about 27 weeks of the year with sittings beginning in September and continuing until June. Each House meets regularly to deal with national issues and debate legislation.

At the beginning of each Parliament following a general election, a Speaker is chosen to preside over each House. The Speaker of the Senate is appointed on the advice of the Prime Minister. In the House of Commons, Members elect by secret ballot one of themselves to be their Speaker.

The Centennial Flame was ignited by Prime Minister Lester B. Pearson on December 31, 1966 to commemorate the 100th anniversary of Confederation. The Centennial Flame includes twelve bronze shields for each of the provinces and territories that existed in 1967, as well as their floral symbol and the date that the province or territory joined Confederation. Nunavut is a new territory created in 1999.

Sir John A. Macdonald (1815-1891) was one of the driving forces behind Confederation in Canada, with Nova Scotia, New Brunswick, Ontario and Quebec joining together to form a new country. Macdonald served as the country's first prime minister. Manitoba, British Columbia and Prince Edward Island entered Confederation under his government, while the last spike of the Canadian Pacific Railway's transcontinental line was hammered into the ground. The monument shown on Page 18 depicts Macdonald ready to engage in a spirited debate, with spectacles in one hand and notes in another. Below him sits a youthful woman symbolizing Confederation; she holds the coat of arms attributed to Canada.

Sir Wilfrid Laurier inspired Canadians to believe in a distinguished future for the nation. His achievements included a vigorous immigration policy to help development in the west, agricultural and industrial progress, and the admission into Confederation of a new territory, Yukon, as well as two new provinces, Alberta and Saskatchewan. He is responsible for making Ottawa a true capital that all Canadians can look upon with pride. He created the Ottawa Improvement Commission in 1899 to beautify and plan the capital.

Queen Elizabeth is Canada's reigning monarch. She signed the *Constitution Act* in 1982 which patriated Canada's constitution from the United Kingdom, and established the Charter of Rights and Freedoms. This completed Canada's peaceful march to full national independence. Prior to this act, major amendments to the Canadian constitution required passage by the British Parliament. Changes can now be made by Canada's Parliament.

The RCMP has become Canada's national police service with a force of over 26,000 men and women active in every province and territory of the country. They are famous for their scarlet coat, Stetson hat and tall leather boots. Their less ceremonial attire is navy blue jackets, vests and pants with a yellow stripe.

The Rideau Canal, a great military engineering achievement of the nineteenth century, was completed in 1832 and opened central Canada to settlement and trade. The canal was planned after the War of 1812 to provide a safe way to transport troops and equipment between Montreal and Kingston. The entrance locks mark the beginning of a 202-kilometer route linking the Ottawa River and Lake Ontario through a system of lakes and rivers connected and made navigable by the channels, locks and dams that the workers constructed. The canal was never used for defence. It was first a commercial, then a recreational waterway.

The Ottawa River flows through Canada's Capital Region separating Ottawa and Gatineau. This waterway played a vital role in their development. For a century and a half, the Capital Region was a hub of the lumber industry and millions of logs were floated downstream on the Ottawa River.

The Bank of Canada is our country's monetary authority. Its purpose is to promote the economic and financial well-being of Canadians. It does this by aiming to keep inflation low, stable and predictable. By setting a target for short-term interest rates, the Bank of Canada influences other rates and, in turn, savings and investment decisions. The Bank also issues Canada's paper currency and works to protect its security. As the federal government's banker, the Bank helps to manage government funds and the public debt.

Parliament Hill

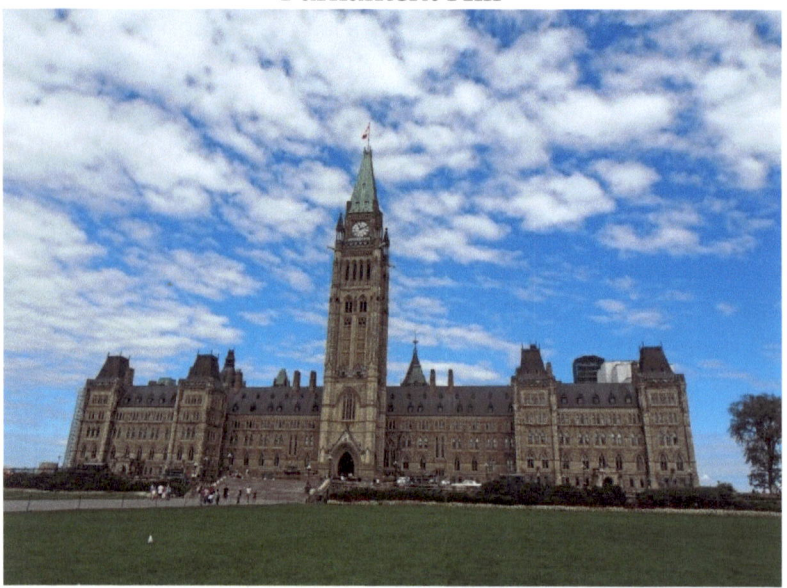

Centre Block with Peace Tower

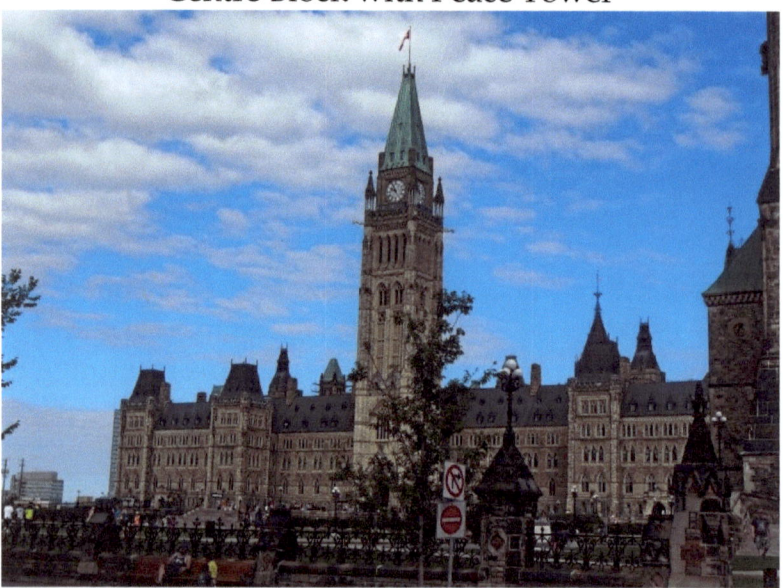

The four-faced clock is modelled after the one in the main tower of the British Parliament in London, England. The chime tune of this electric clock is played upon five of the bells of the carillon. The largest bell, the bourdon, strikes the hour.

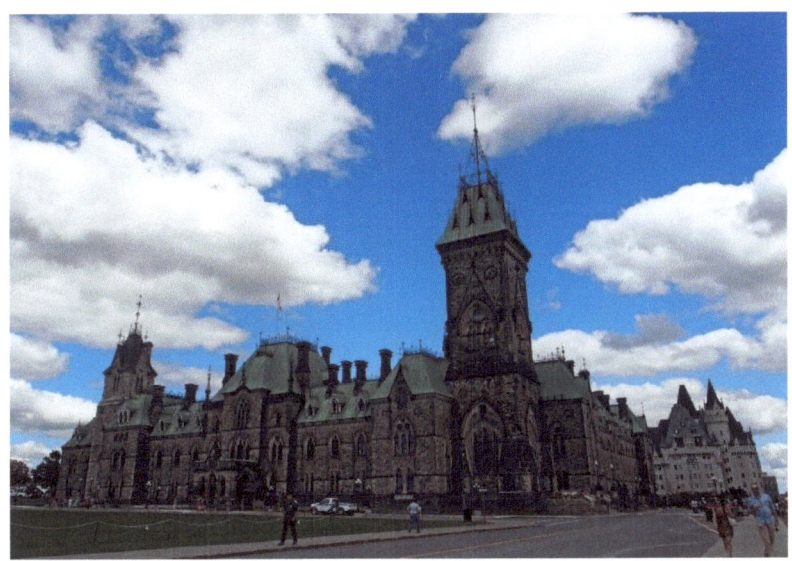

East Block

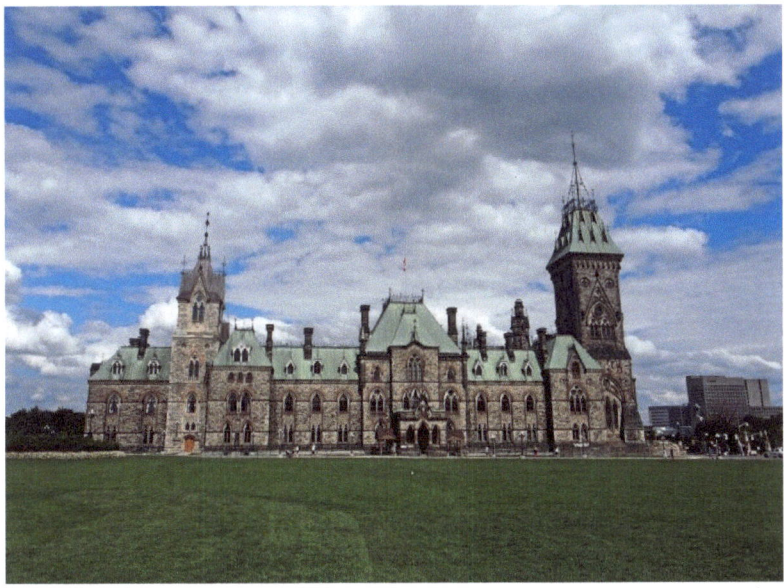

The roofs of the Parliament Buildings are copper plated; the green colour is the result of a chemical reaction caused by the copper coming into contact with oxygen and other weathering agents (like rain and pollution).

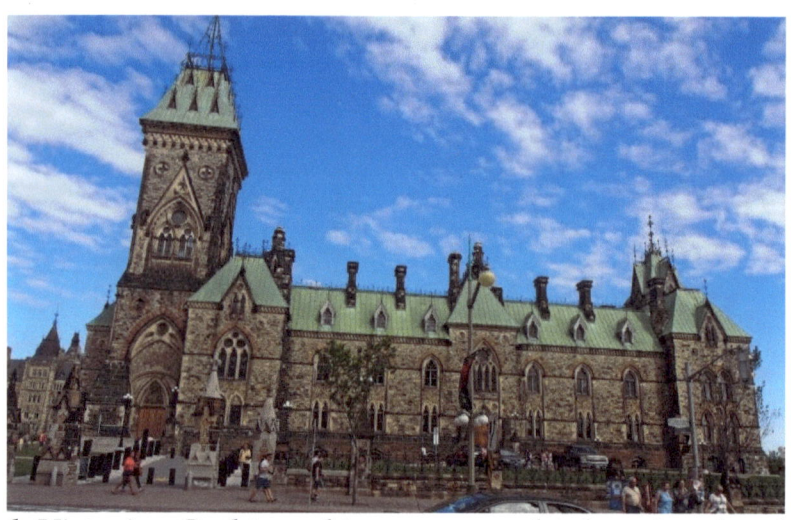

High Victorian Gothic architecture – multiple pointed arches, stones of irregular shape and tone, and intricate masonry and stone carvings

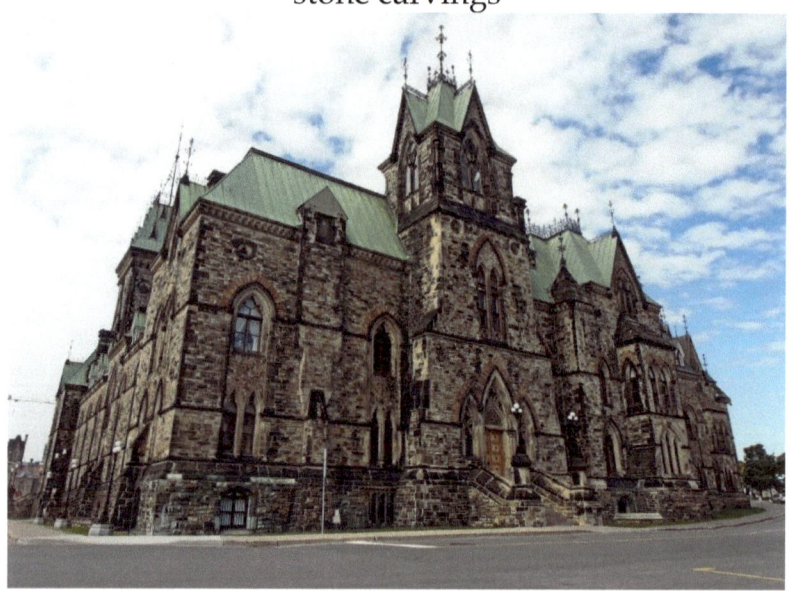

The outer walls of the Parliament Buildings are made of local Nepean sandstone, a porous stone that reacts with the pollution in the air. Once a pale beige colour, the stones have turned black over the years.

War of 1812 Monument – *Triumph Through Diversity*

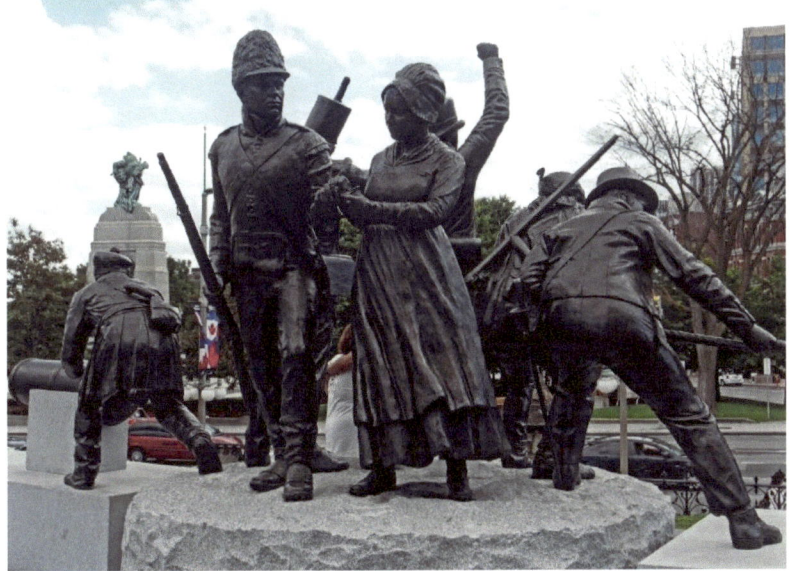

A woman bandaging the arm of a Voltigeur, a Royal Navy
sailor pulling a rope

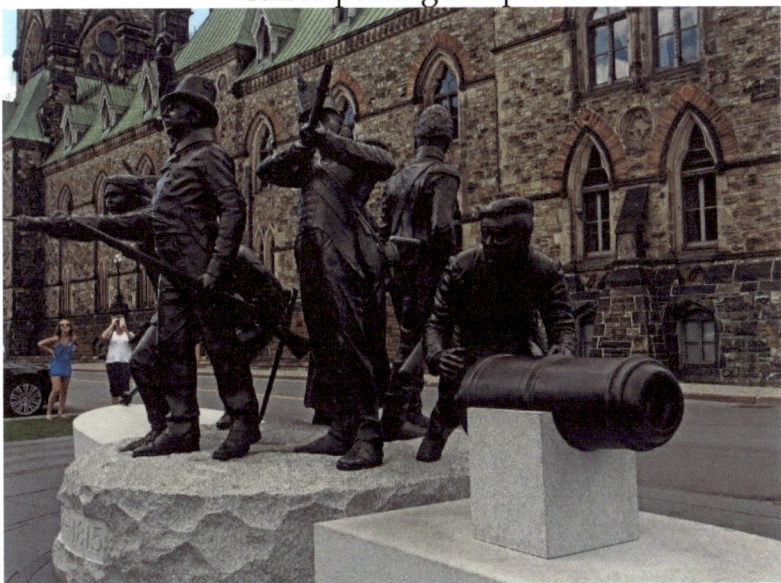

The rough-hewn base on which the seven figures are standing
represents the ruggedness of the land in the 1800s.

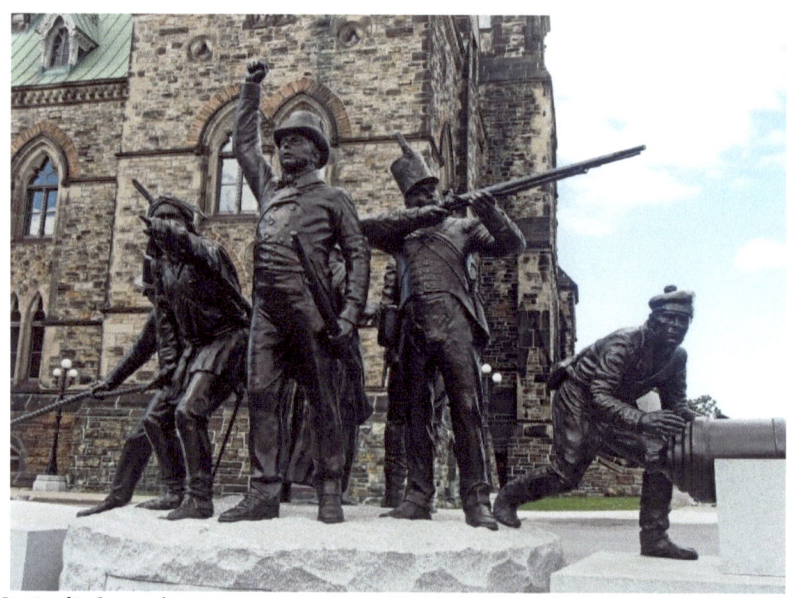

A Metis fighter firing a cannon, a British Regular aiming a musket, a Canadian militiaman raising his arm in triumph, a First Nation warrior pointing to the distance

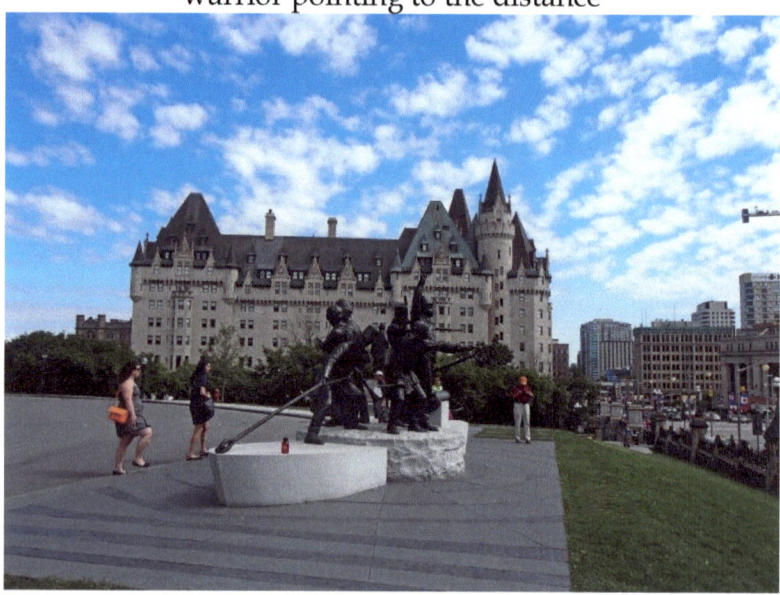

A lasting tribute to the courage and bravery of those who served their country and successfully defended their land from the American invasion

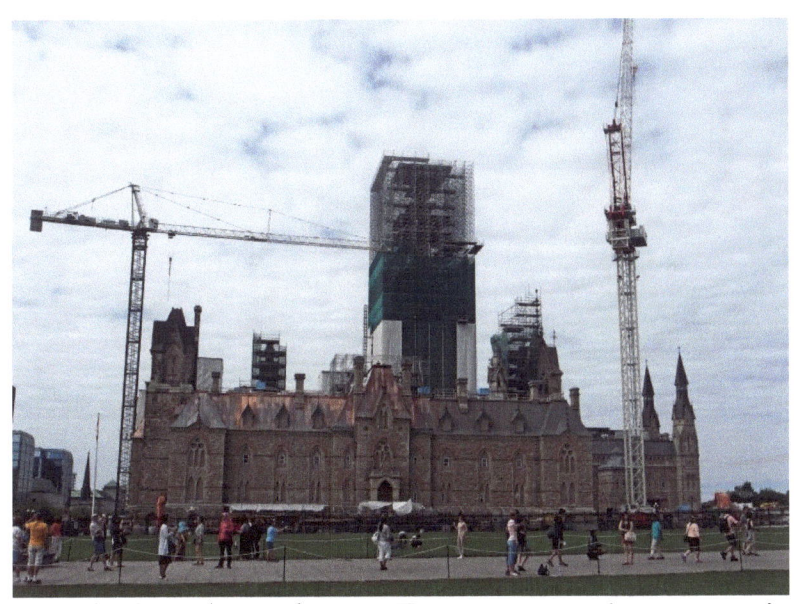

West Block with Mackenzie Tower renovations occurring

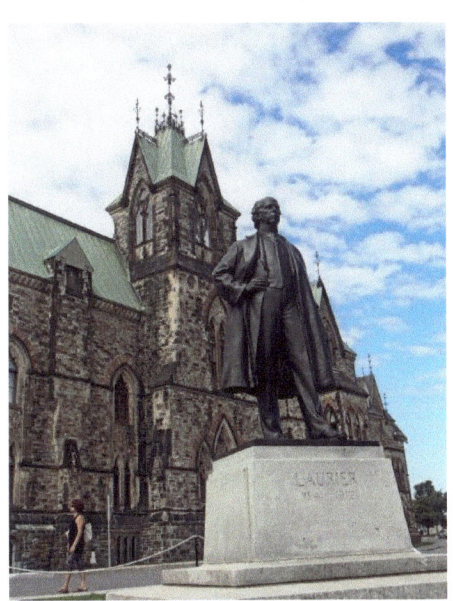

Sir Wilfrid Laurier (1841-1919), 7th Prime Minister of Canada
1896-1911

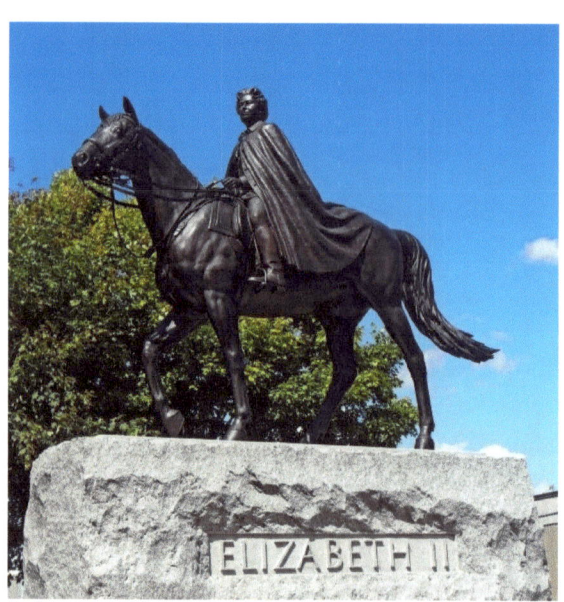

Statue of Queen Elizabeth II – she is depicted on her horse
Centenial, a gift by the RCMP in 1977 to celebrate the 25th
anniversary of her reign; Centenial was named in honor of the
RCMP's 100th anniversary in 1973

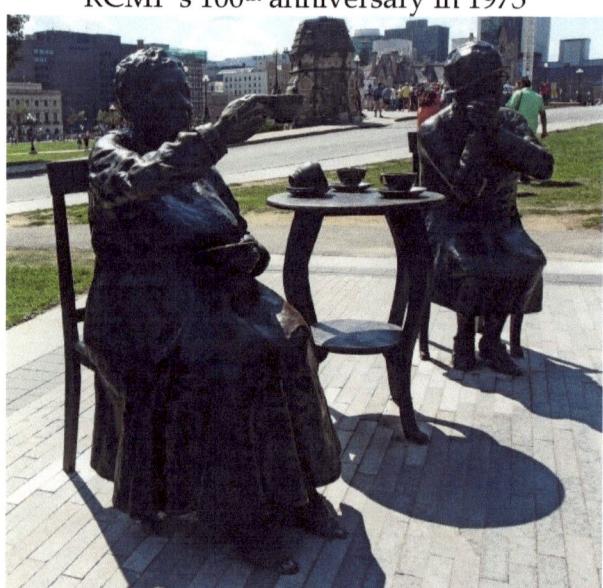

Women are Persons – making them eligible for appointment to the
Senate

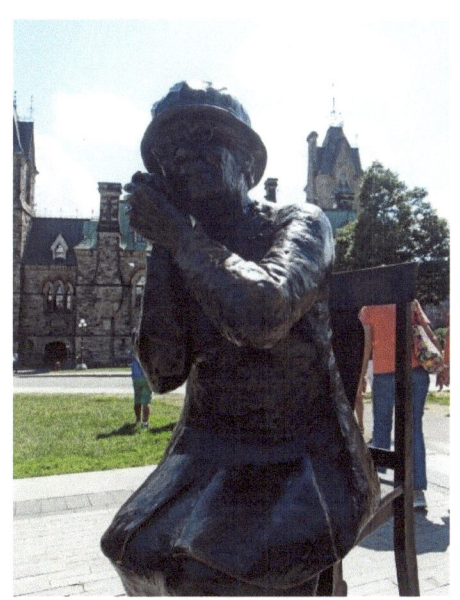
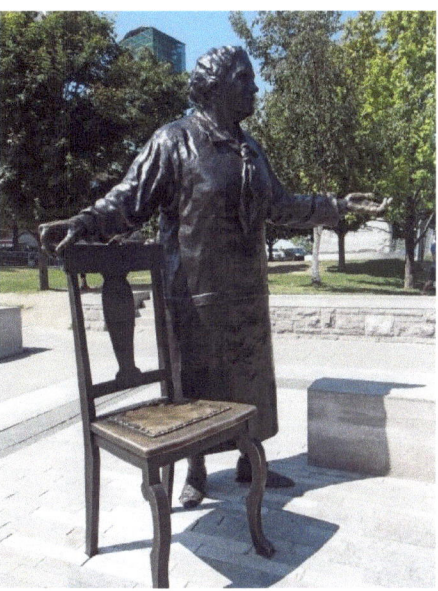

Five women were involved in bringing about this change: Nellie McClung, Louise McKinney, Emily Murphy, Henrietta Muir Edwards and Irene Parlby

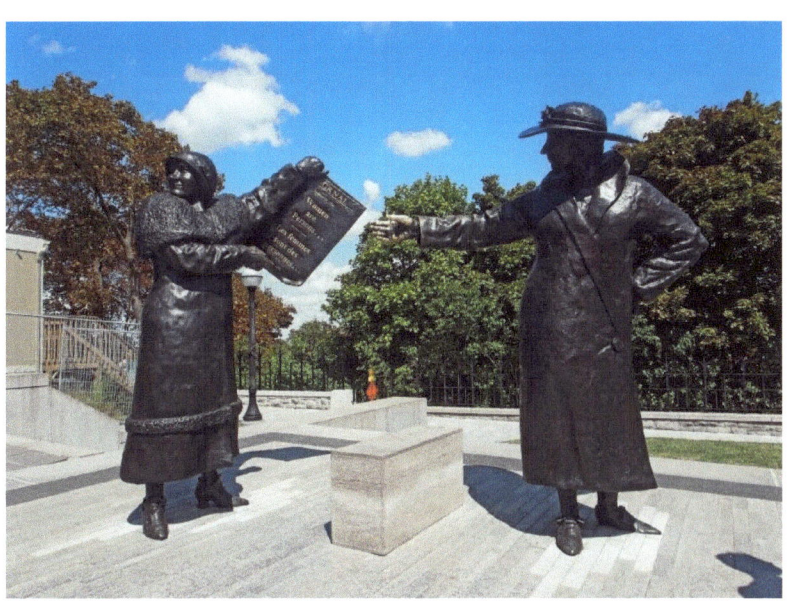

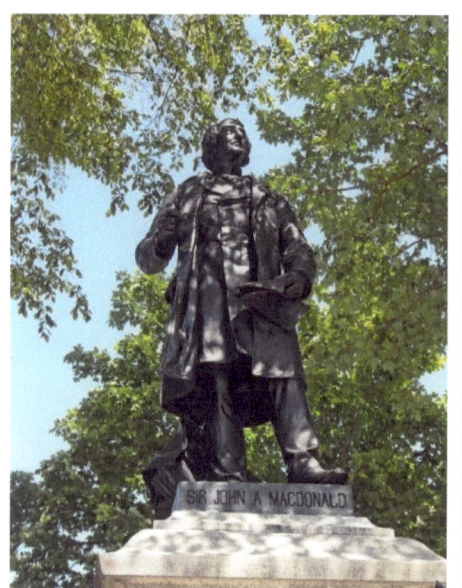
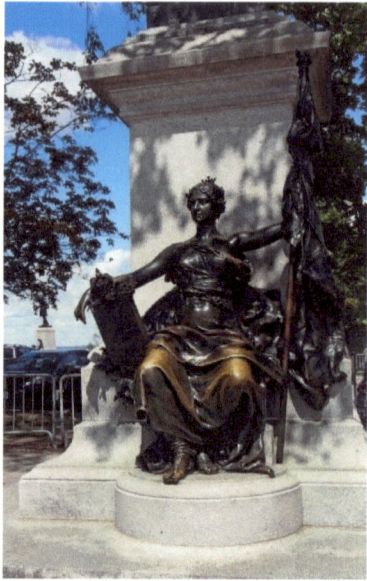

Sir John A. Macdonald with a youthful woman
sitting below - symbolizing Confederation

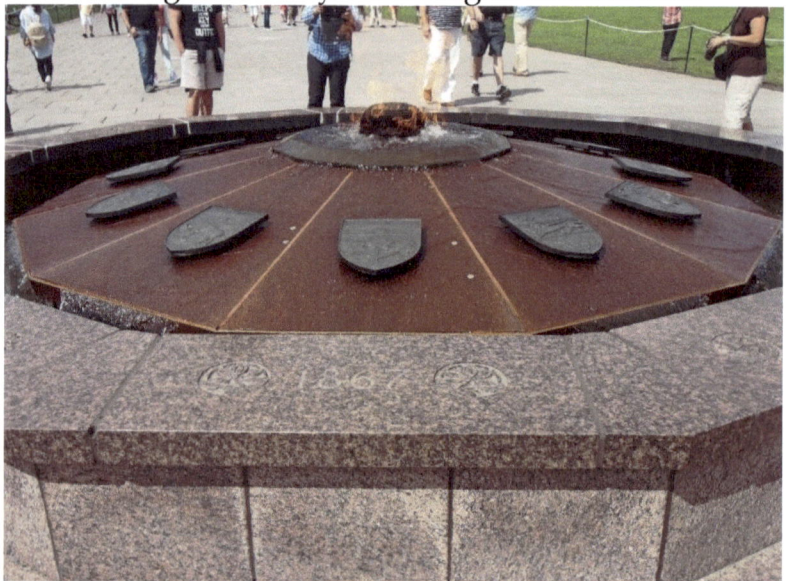

Centennial Flame – natural gas feeds the flame which dances
above the flowing water

Inside the Centre Block

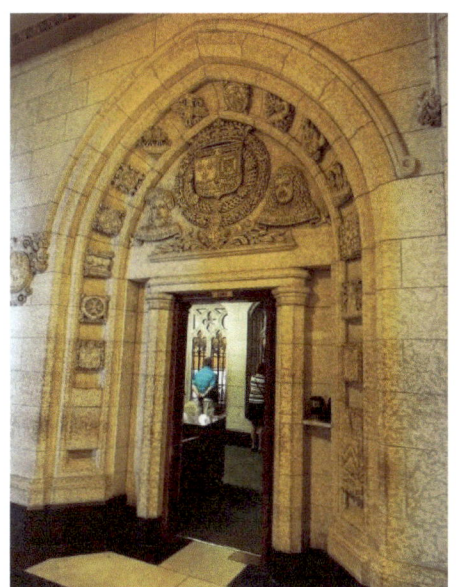

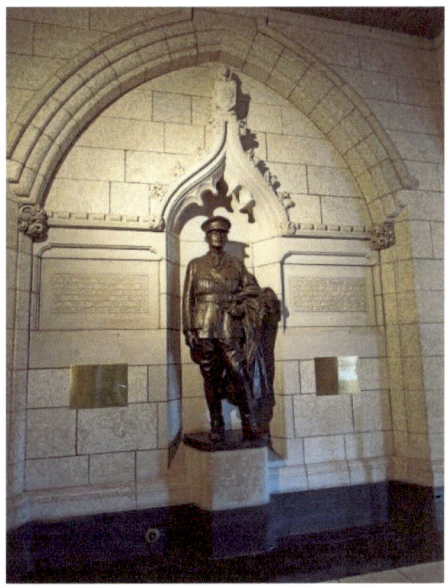

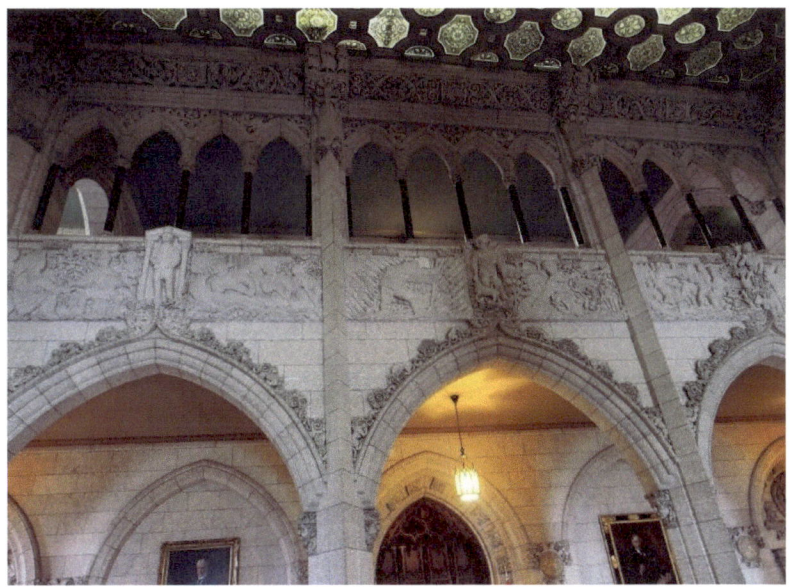

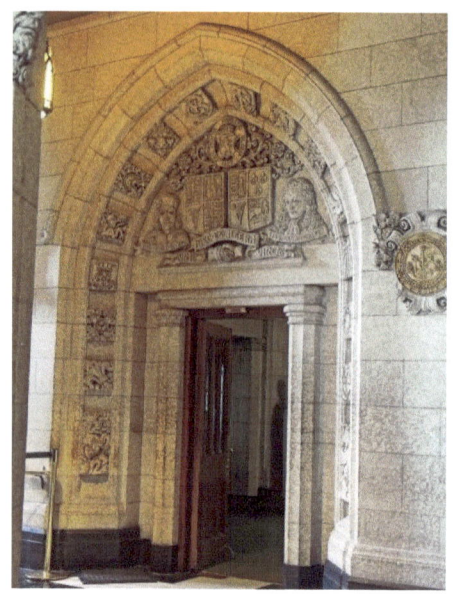
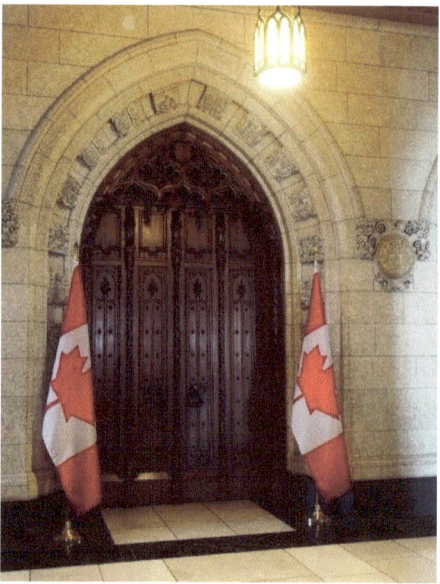

Each doorway has different carvings and crests

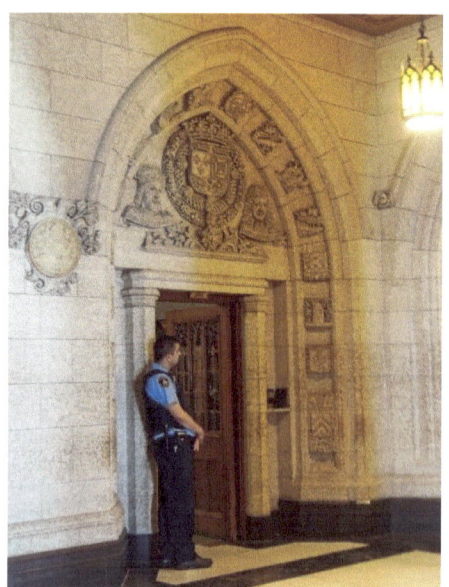
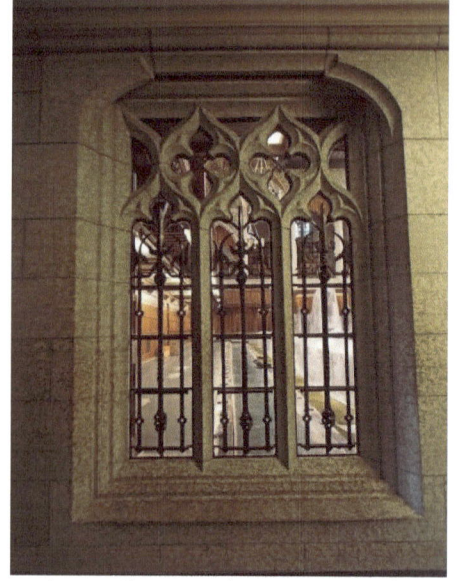

A peak into the House of Commons

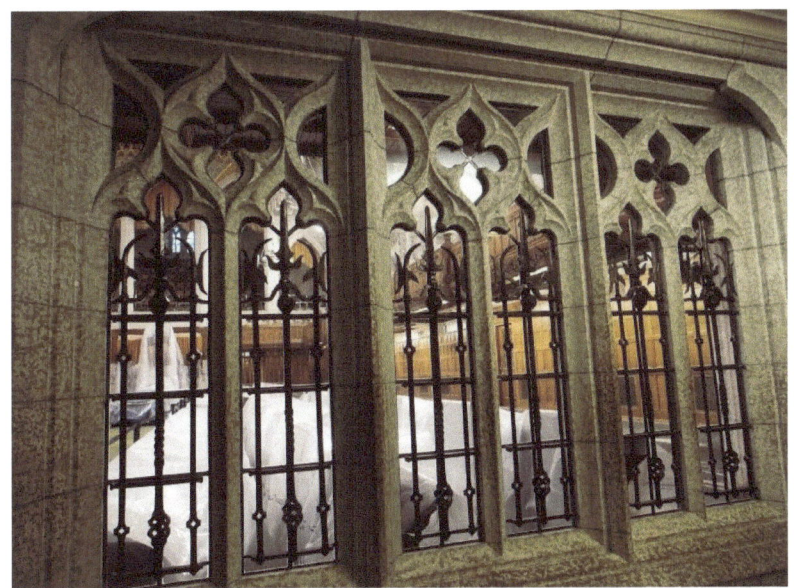

The House of Commons Chamber – decorated in green in the tradition of the British House of Commons; the rectangular Chamber is made of white oak and Tyndall limestone from Manitoba; the stone's freckled surface contains old fossils.

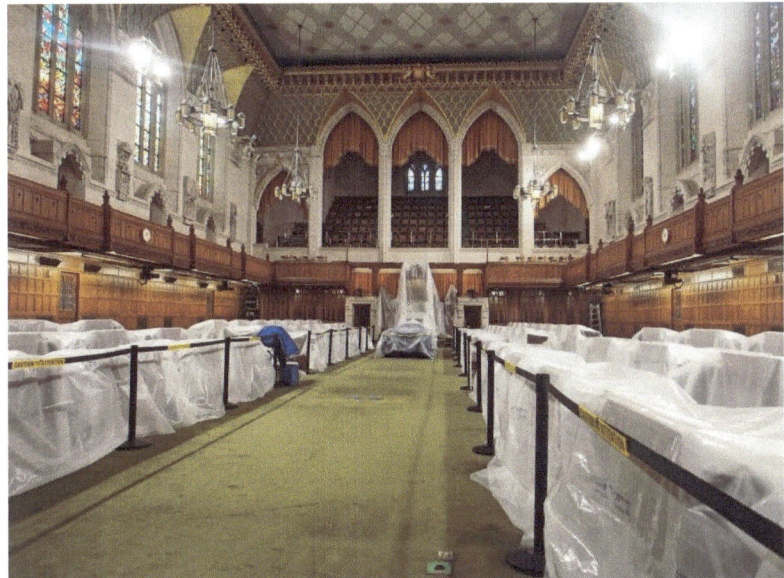

In the process of making it larger to hold more Members of Parliament

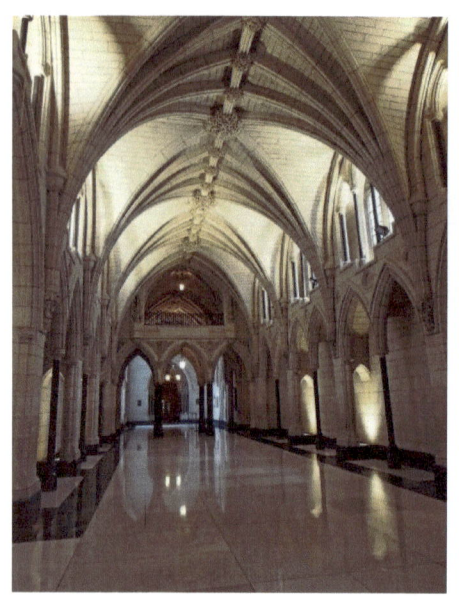
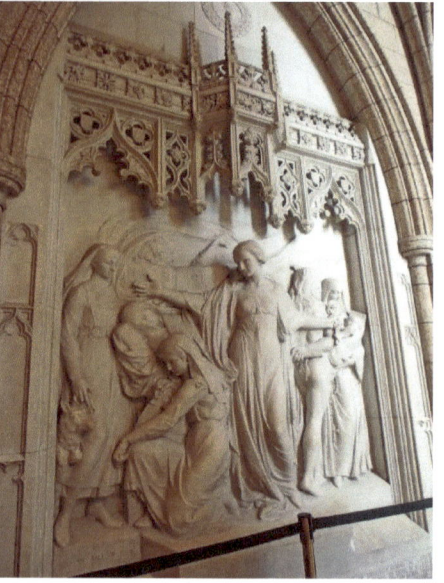
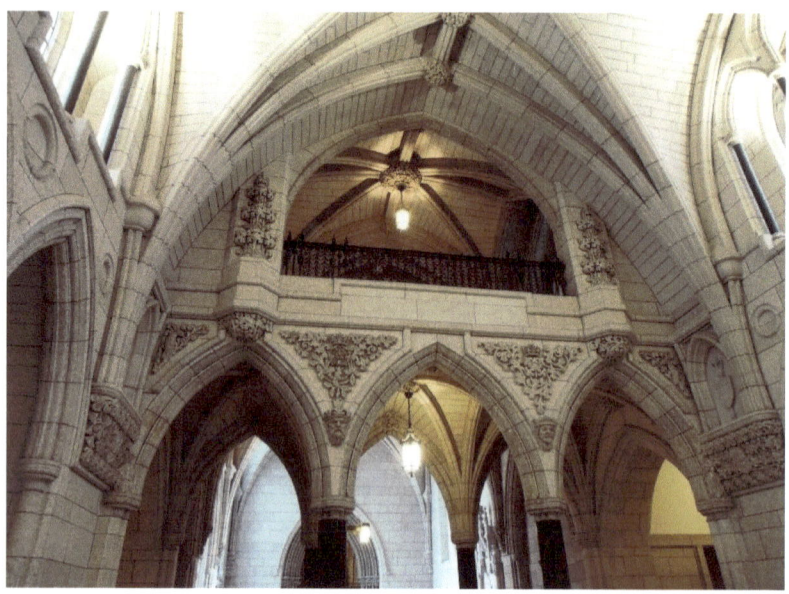

Library of Parliament

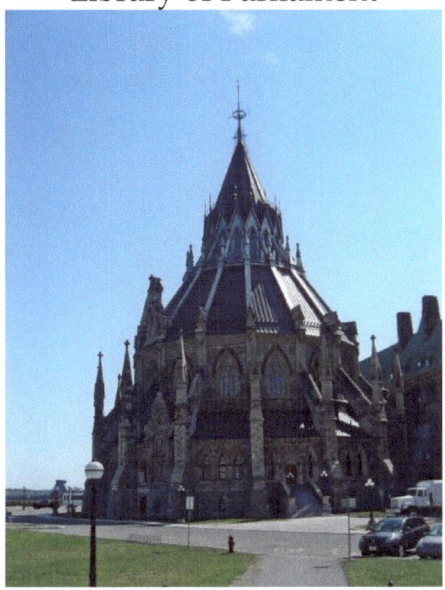

Gothic Revival – flying buttresses, rough exterior of Nepean sandstone – looks as if it was hewn from the craggy bluff separating it from the Ottawa River

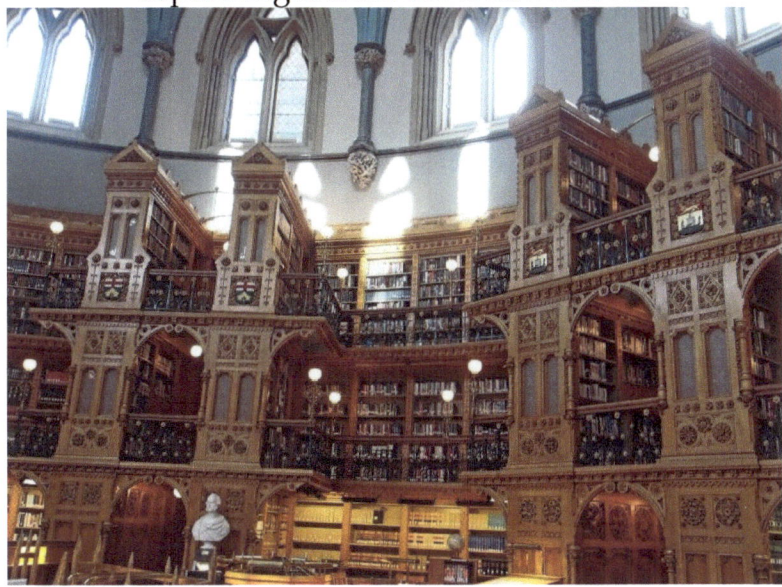

A showpiece of High Victorian Gothic Revival architecture – opened in 1876

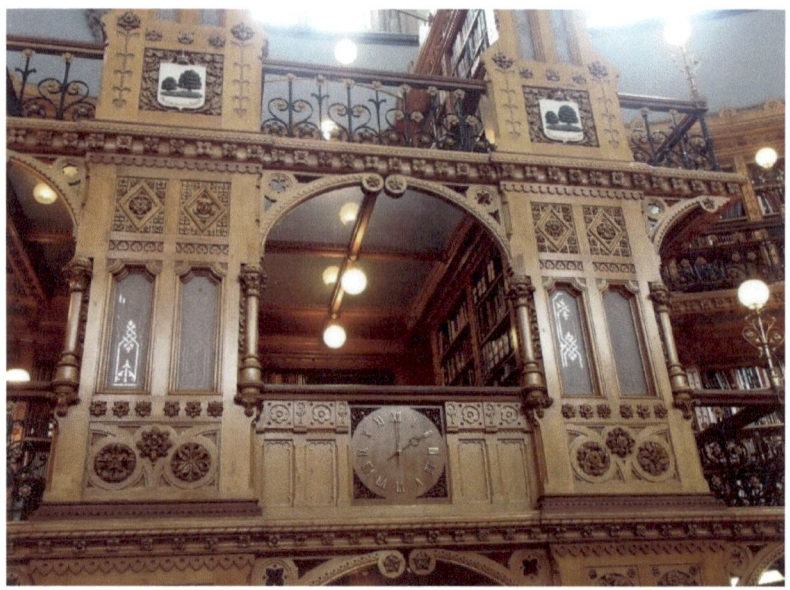

Circular in shape with the use of galleries and alcoves

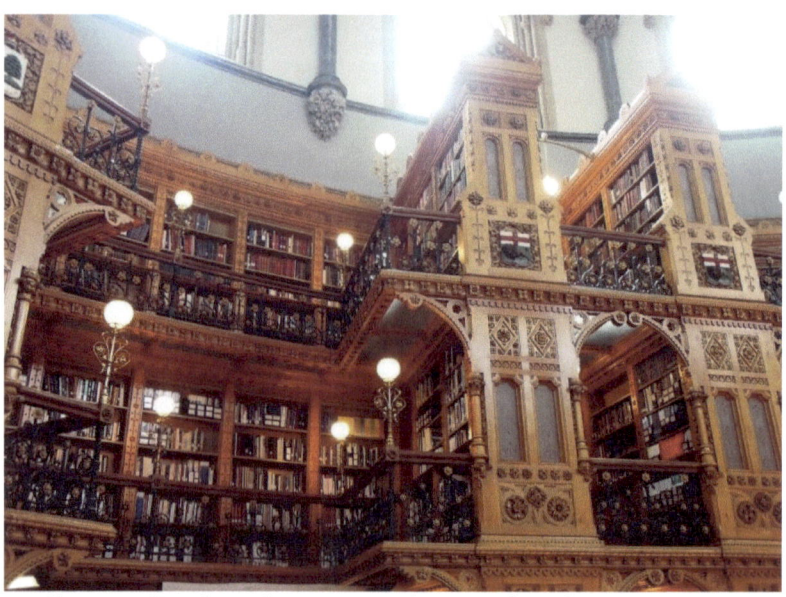

The galleries display the coats of arms for the seven provinces existing in 1876 and one for the Dominion of Canada.

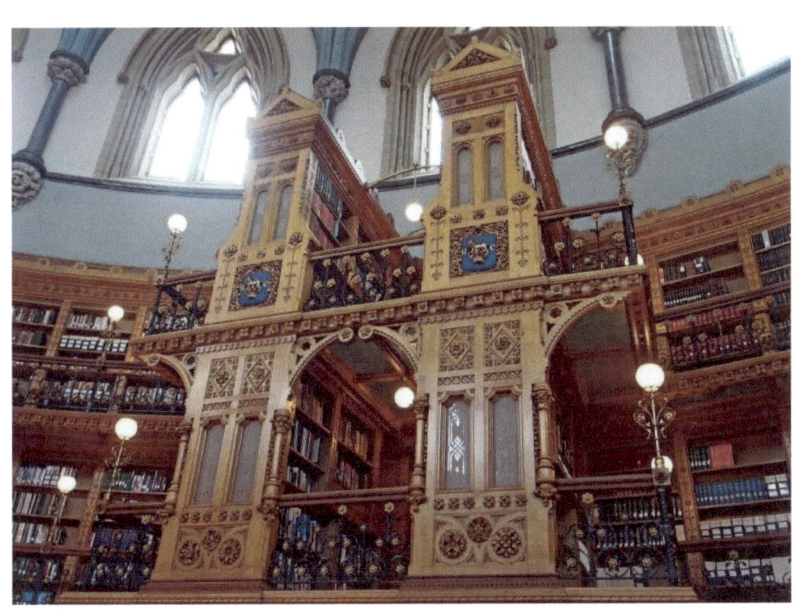

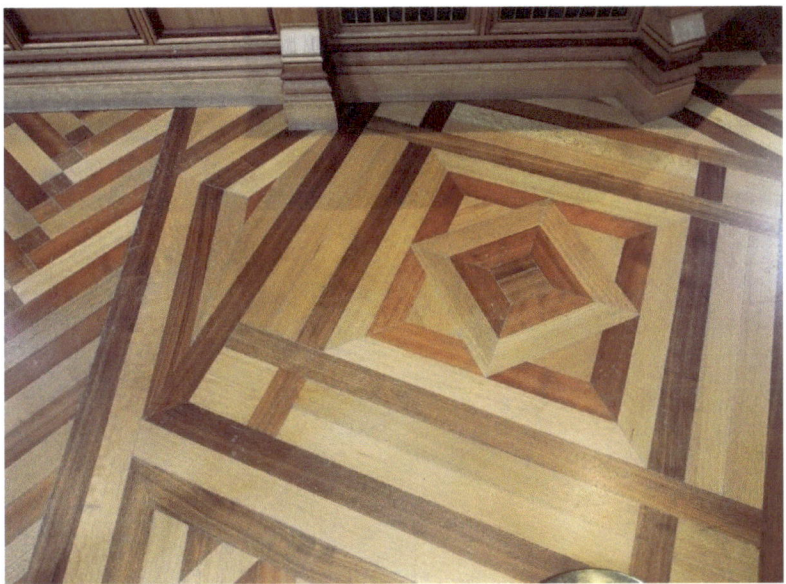

Floor of library – beautiful pattern of cherry, oak and walnut

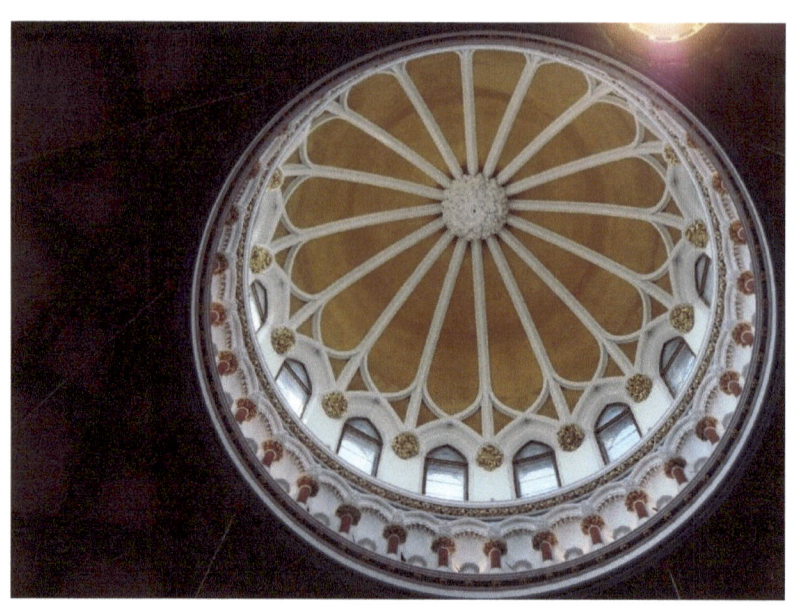

Library ceiling

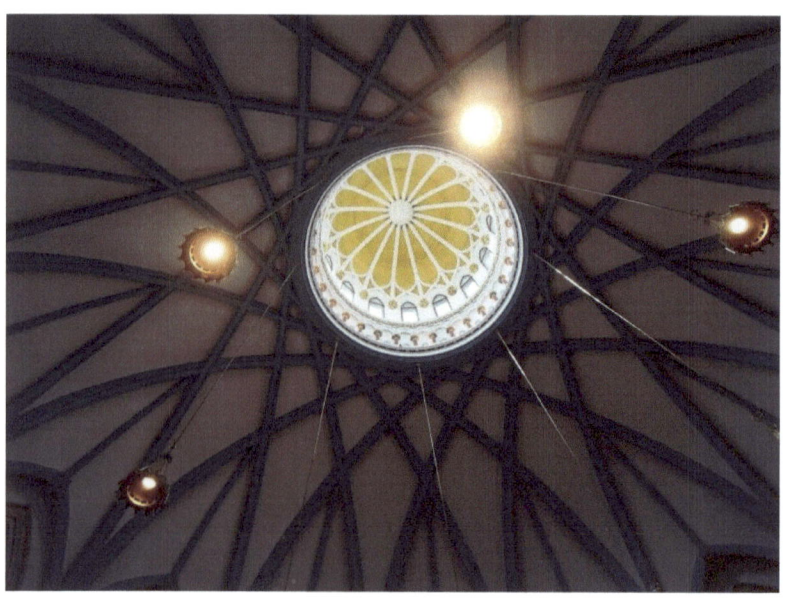

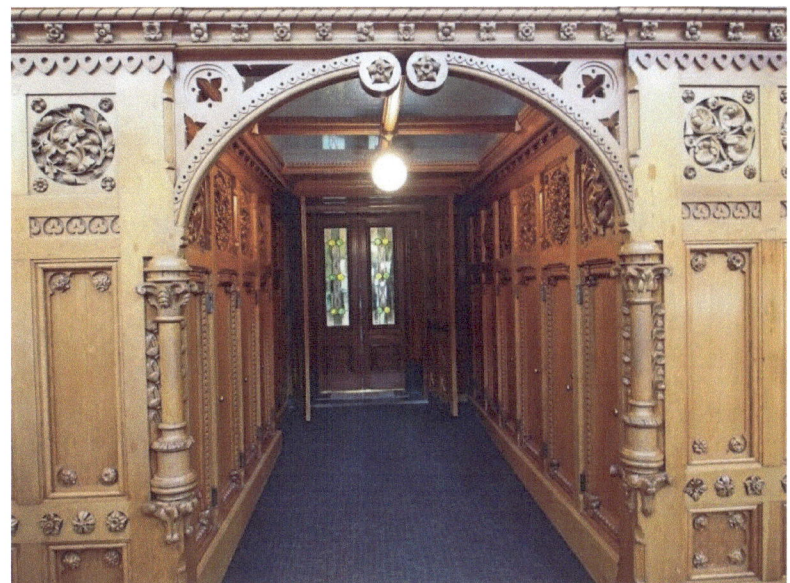

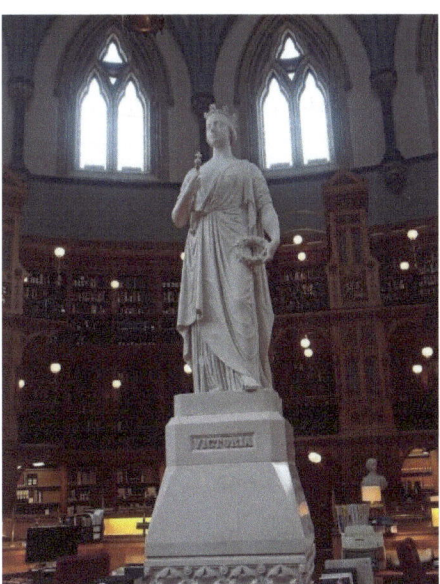
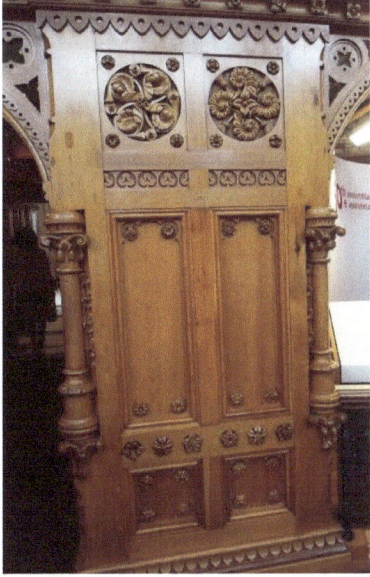

In the centre of the circular domed room stands a white marble statue of the young Queen Victoria sculpted by Marshall Wood in 1871.

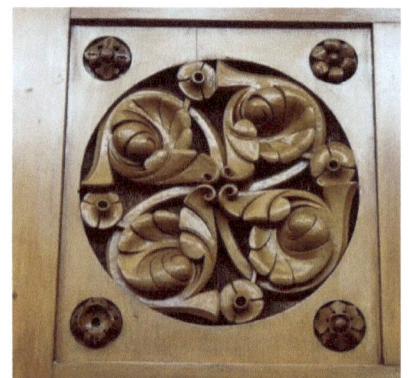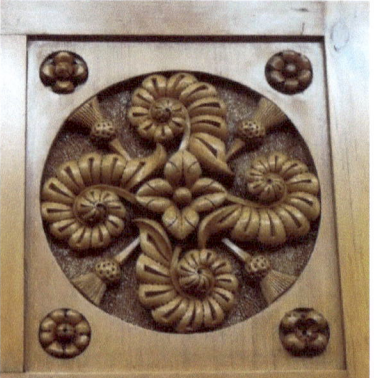

Hundreds of flowers, masks and mythical creatures

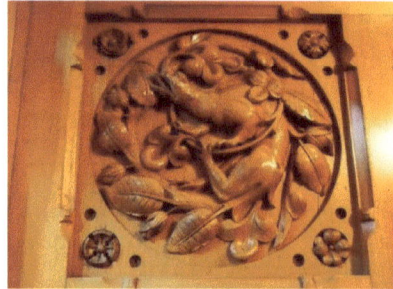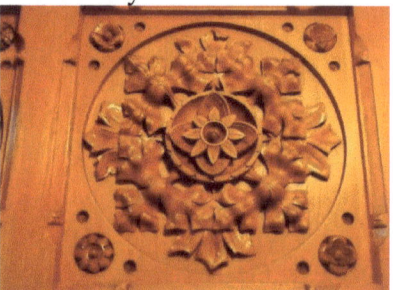

are carved in the white pine panelling

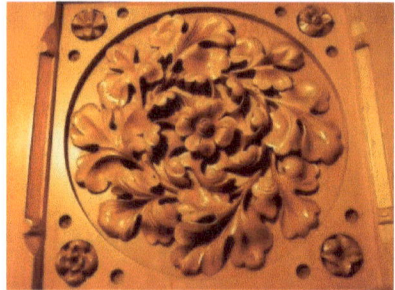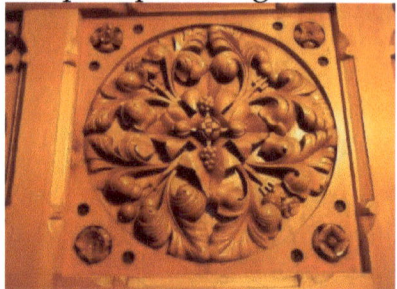

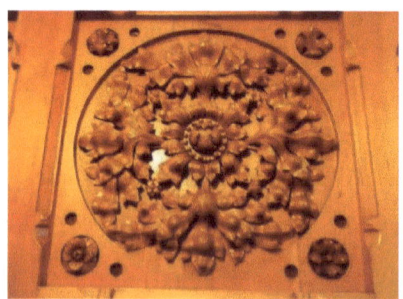

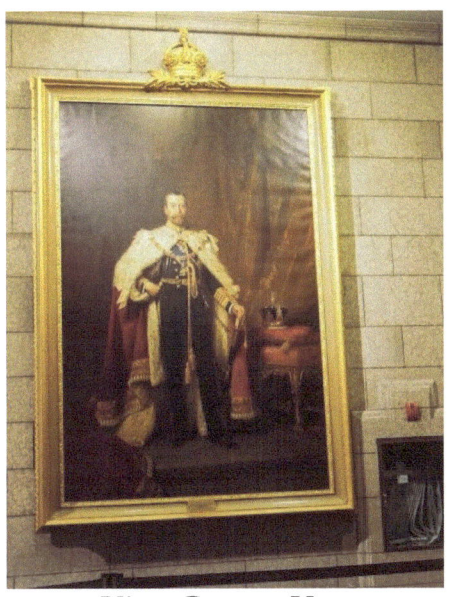

King George V

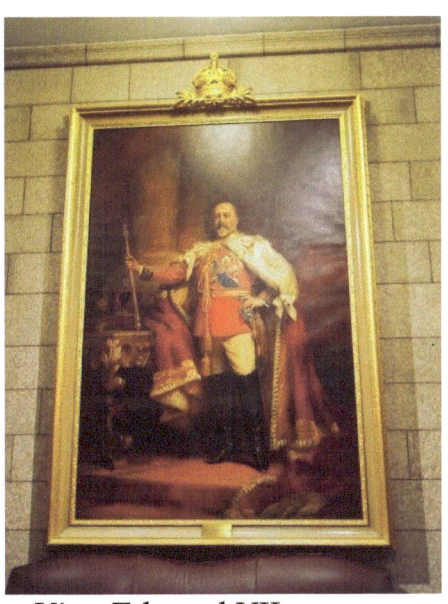

King Edward VII

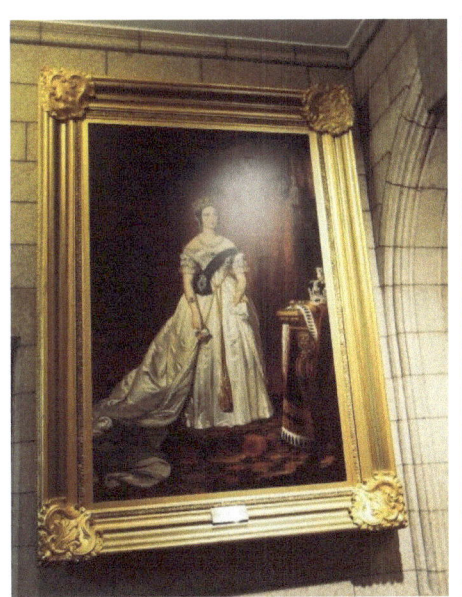

Queen Victoria

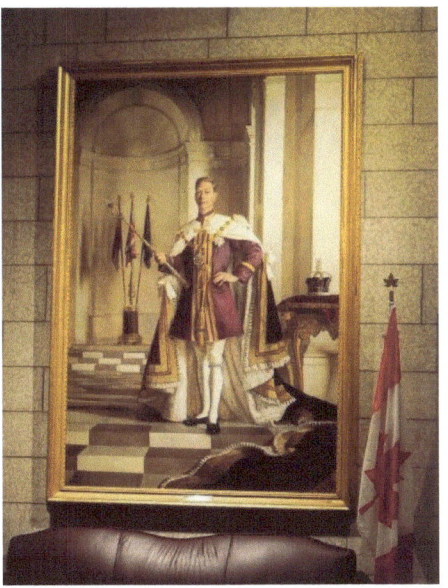

King George VI

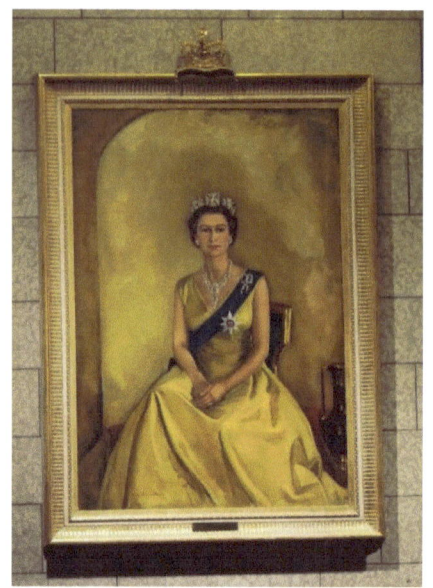
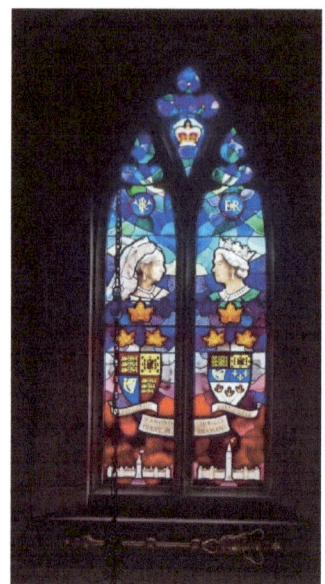

Queen Elizabeth II

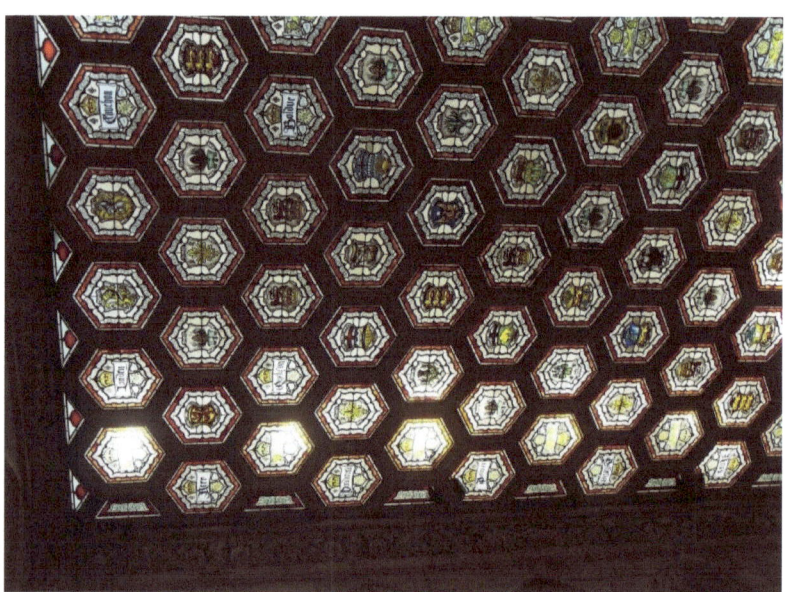

Ceiling

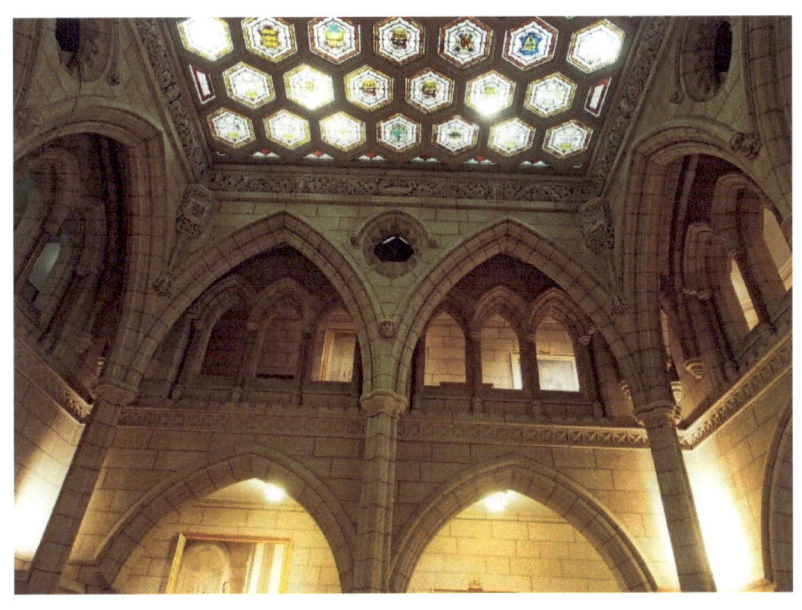

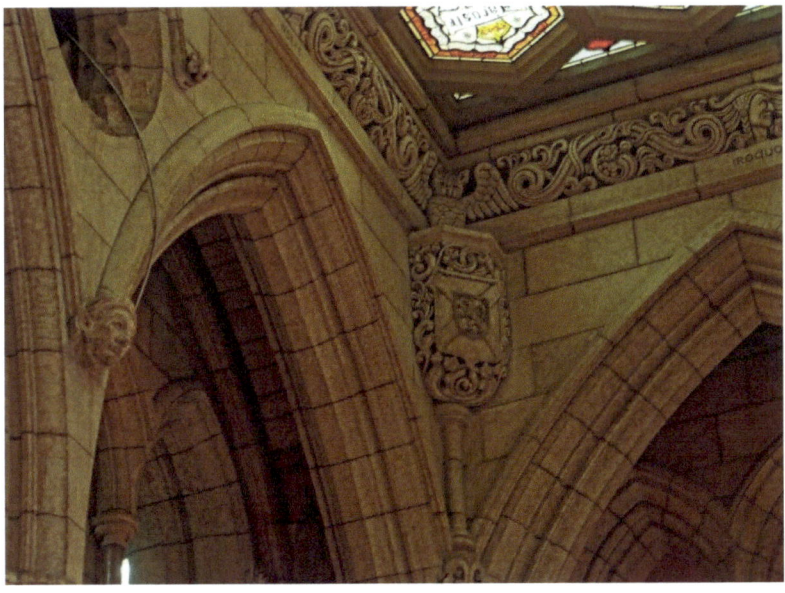

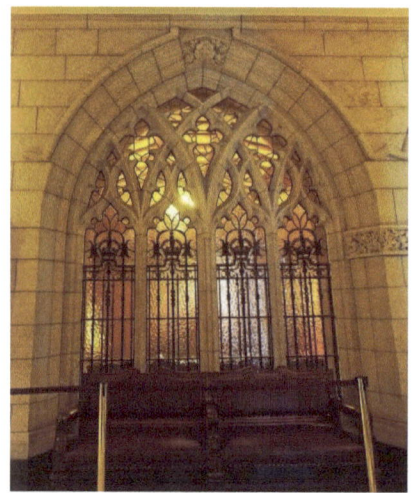

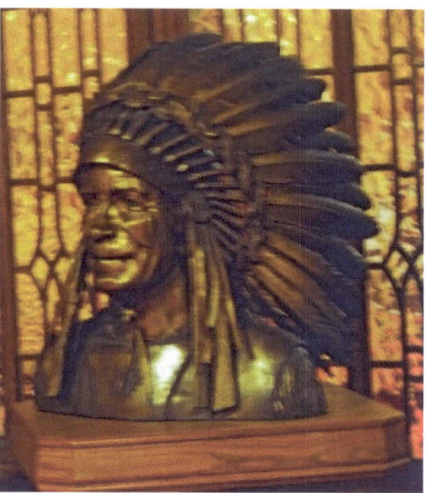

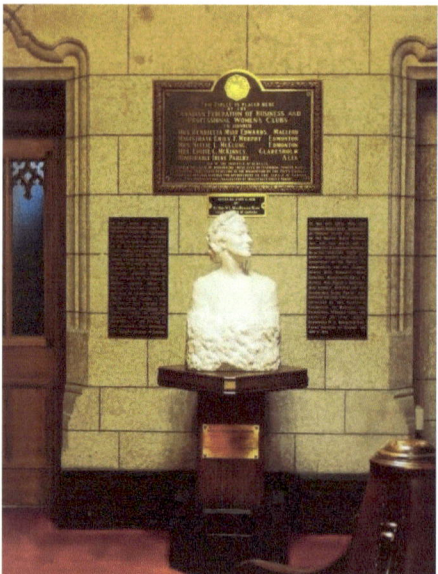

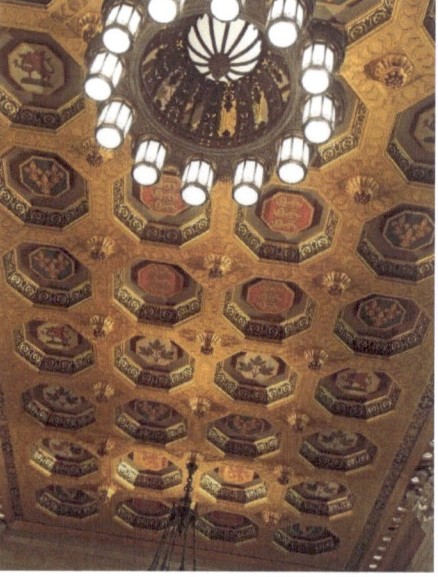

It was not until 1929 that women were recognized as "persons within the meaning of the British North America Act and became eligible for appointment to the Senate.

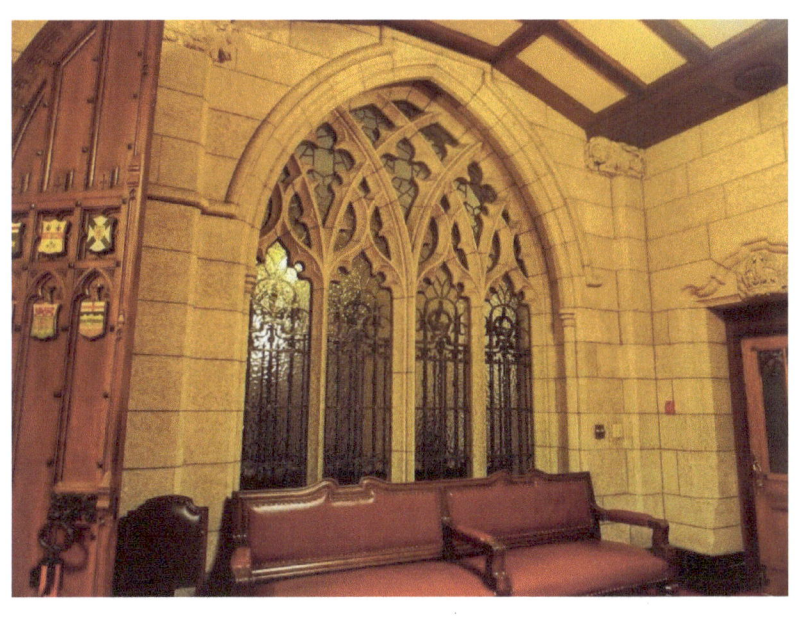

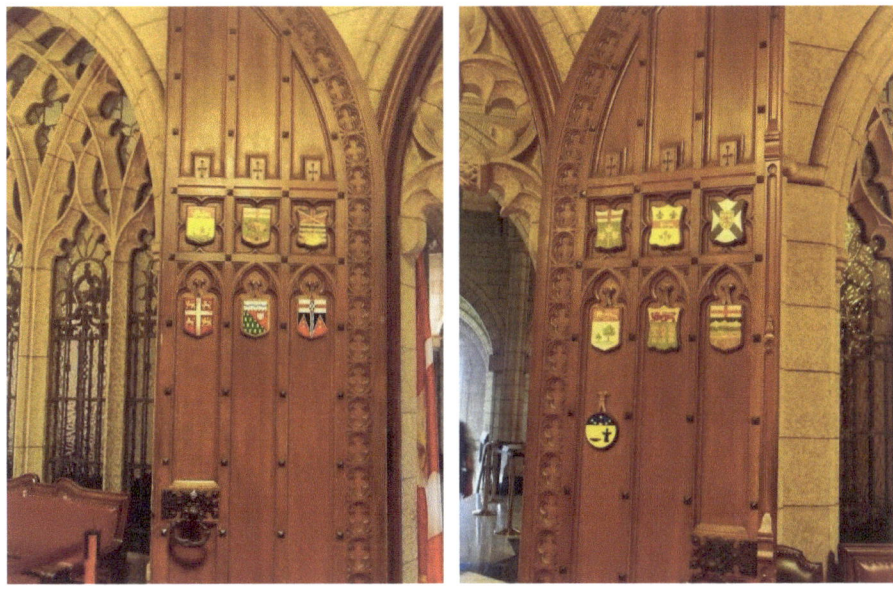

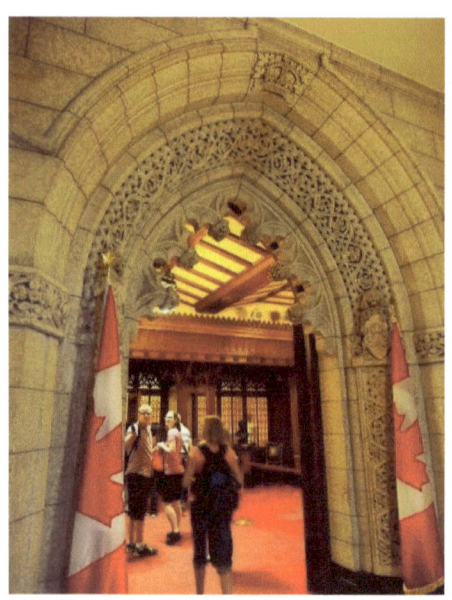 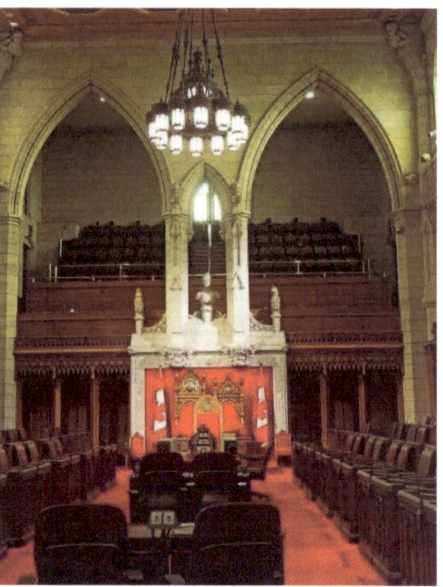

The Senate – red carpeting and upholstery, ceiling with gold leaf – create an air of regal splendour to signify the place where our Head of State meets Parliament.

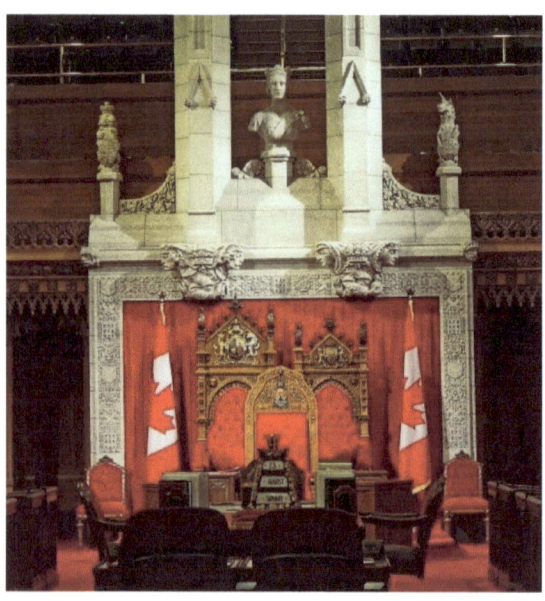

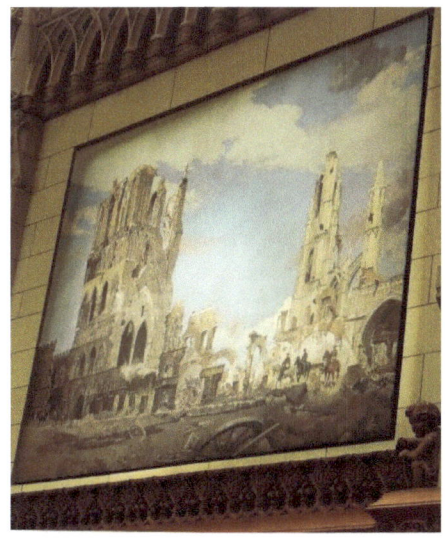

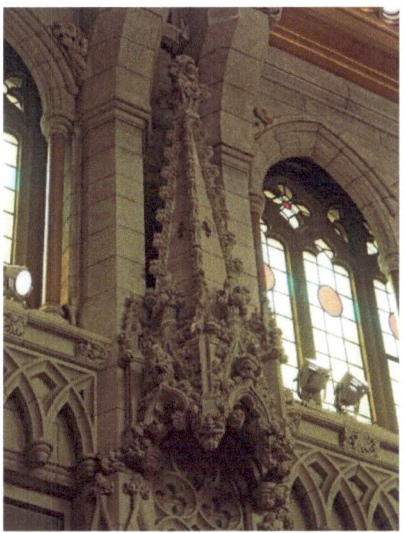

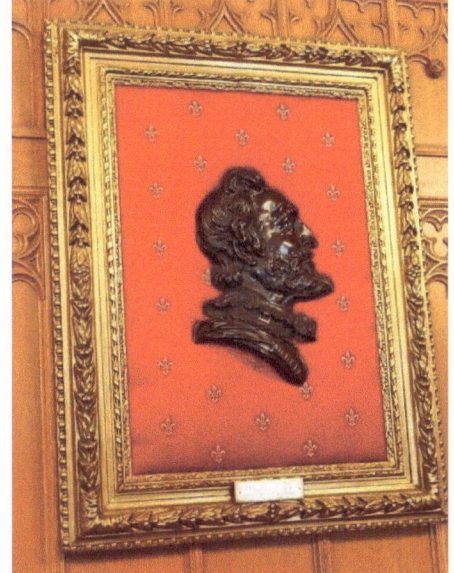

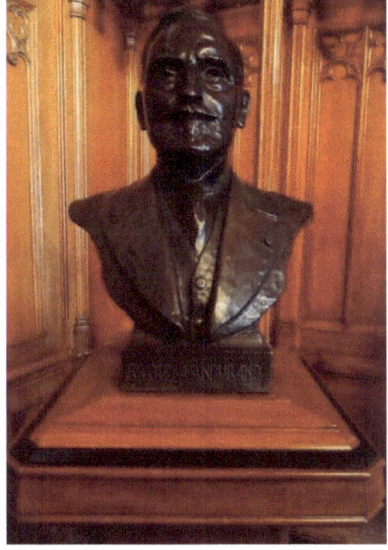

Henry IV

Raoul Dandurand - a Montreal lawyer, appointed to the Senate in 1898 by Sir Wilfrid Laurier; he served as Speaker of the Canadian Senate from 1905-1909.

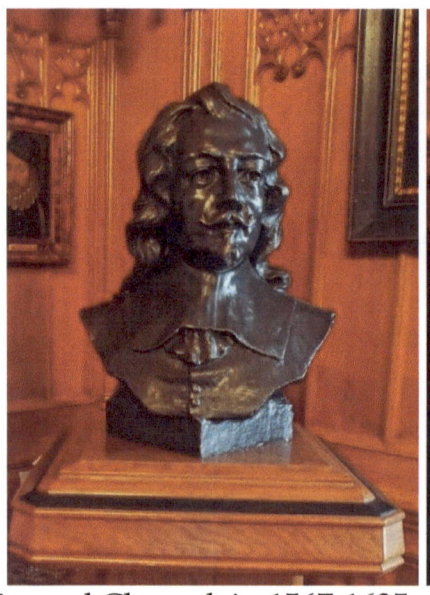 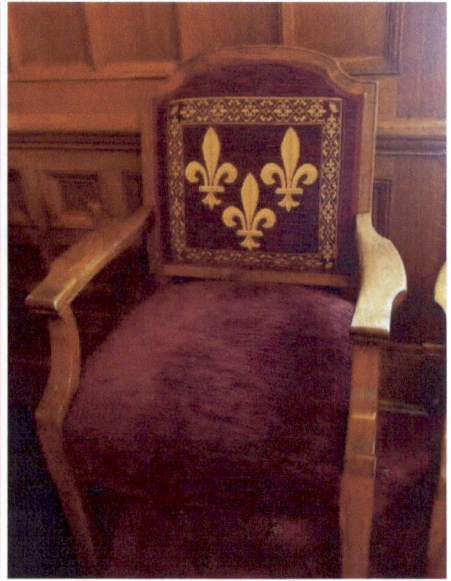

Samuel Champlain 1567-1635
On June 26, 1604, he founded Acadia, the first permanent
French settlement in Canada. In 1608, he founded Quebec.

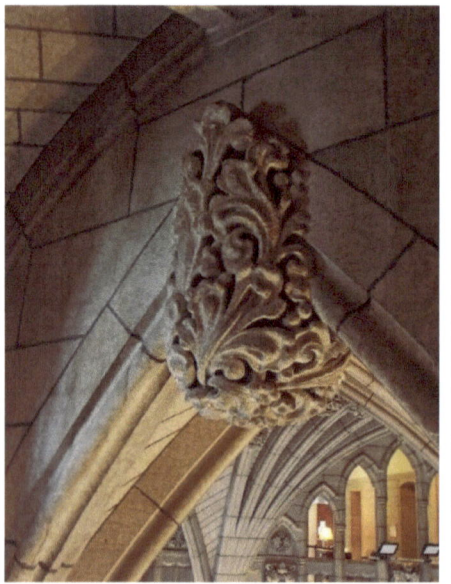 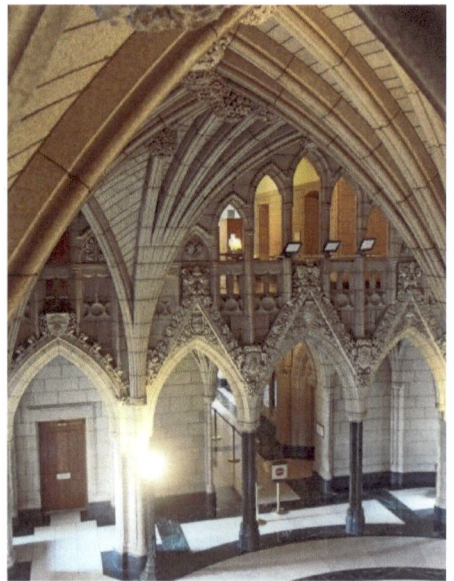

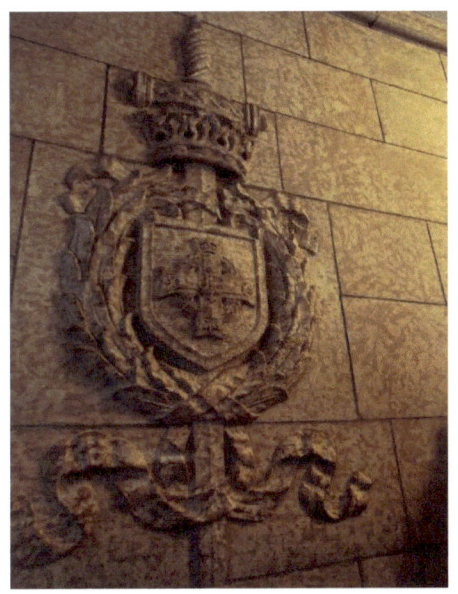

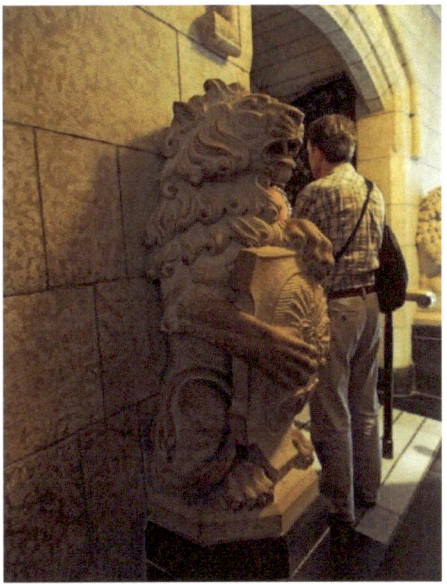

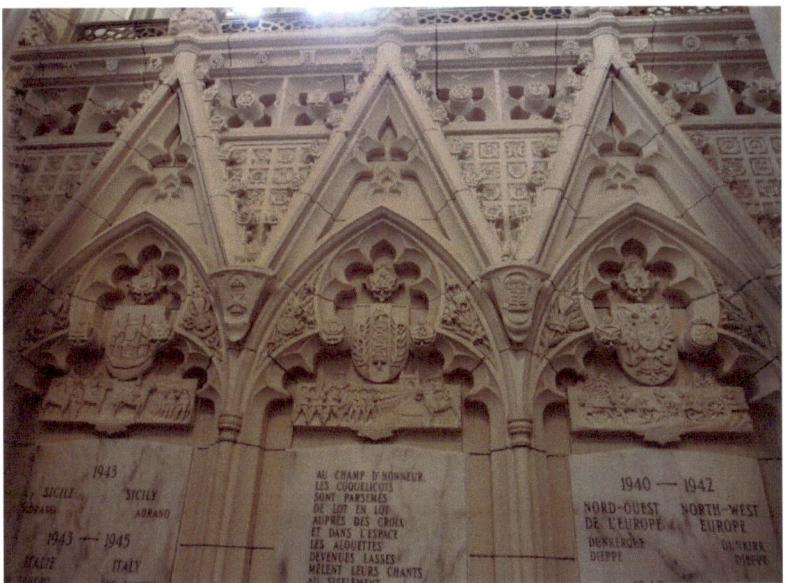

Memorial Chamber

Views from the observation area of the Peace Tower

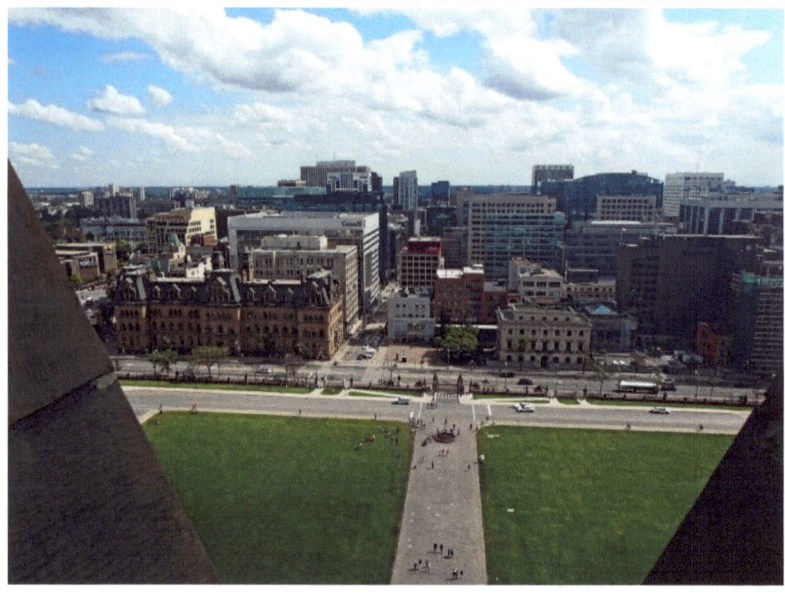

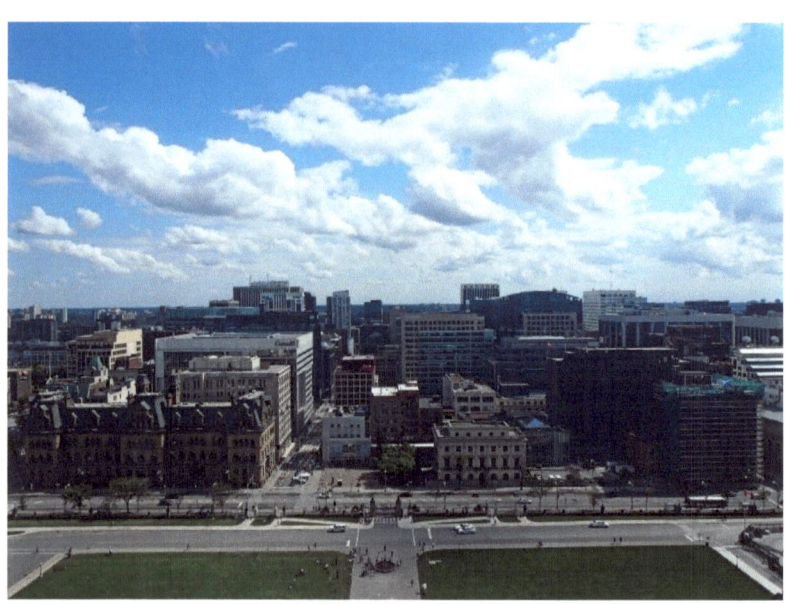

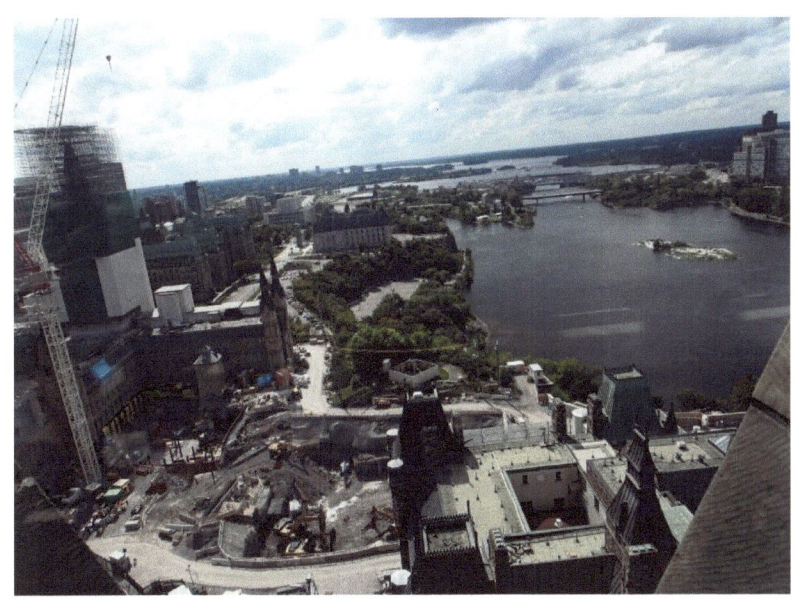

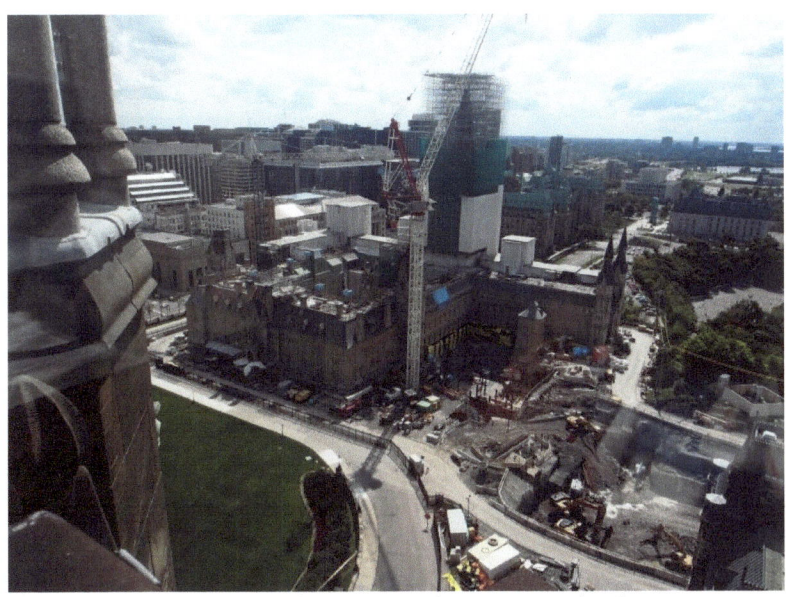

Looking down on the West Block

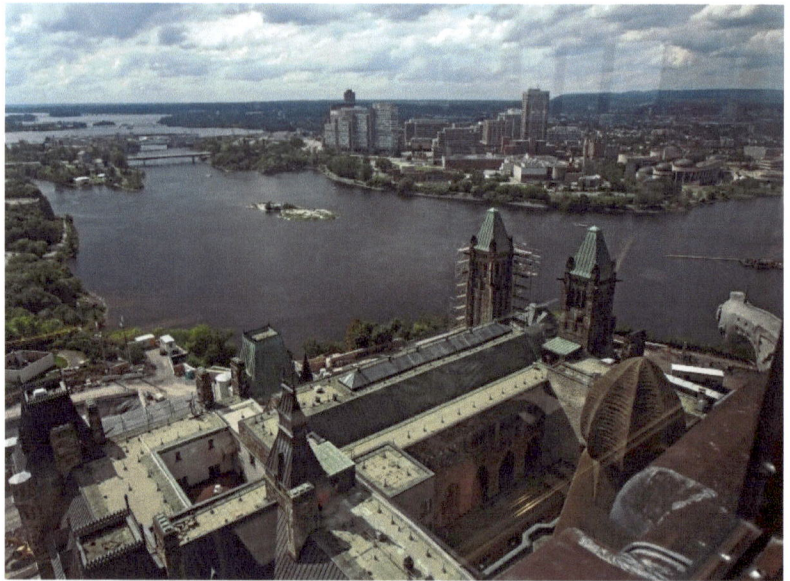

Looking down on the Centre Block

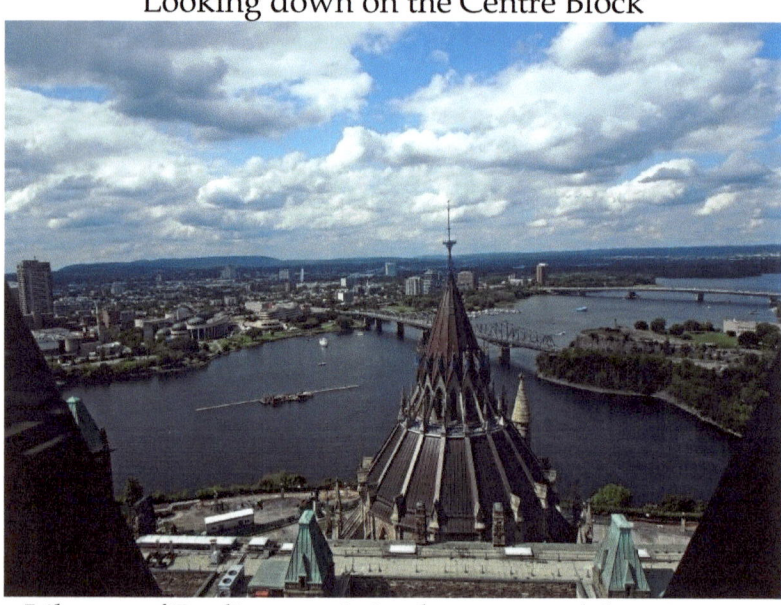

The Library of Parliament is in the centre of the picture with
the Alexandra Bridge, and the Macdonald-Cartier Bridge to
the right which cross the Ottawa River.

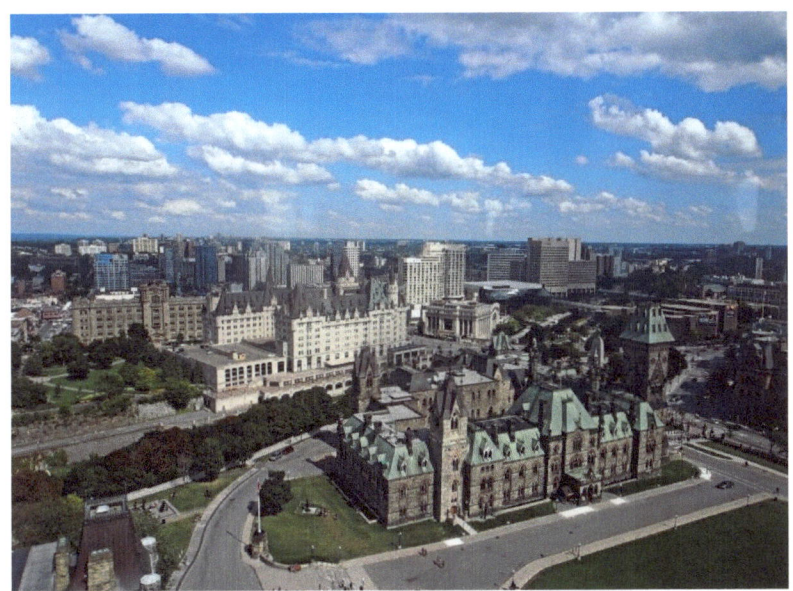

Looking down on the East Block with Chateau Laurier behind - Gothic – lancet arches, trefoils, tracery; Baroque – iron cresting; and Chateau – steeply pitched roofs, and dormers

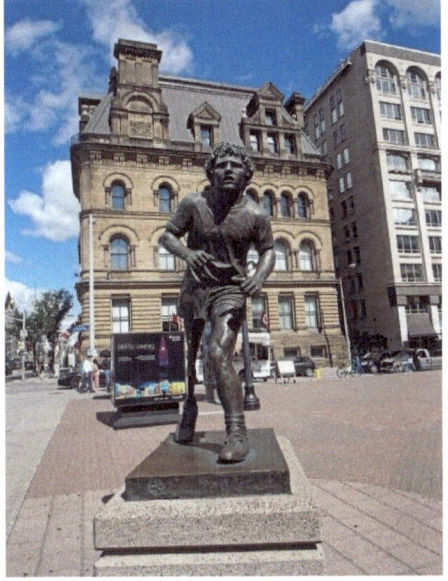

Terry Fox – lost a leg to cancer at age 18; three years later with an artificial leg, he began his cross-Canada run to raise money for cancer research. His journey ended near Thunder Bay, 143 days later – his cancer had returned. He died on June 28, 1981.

Wellington Street

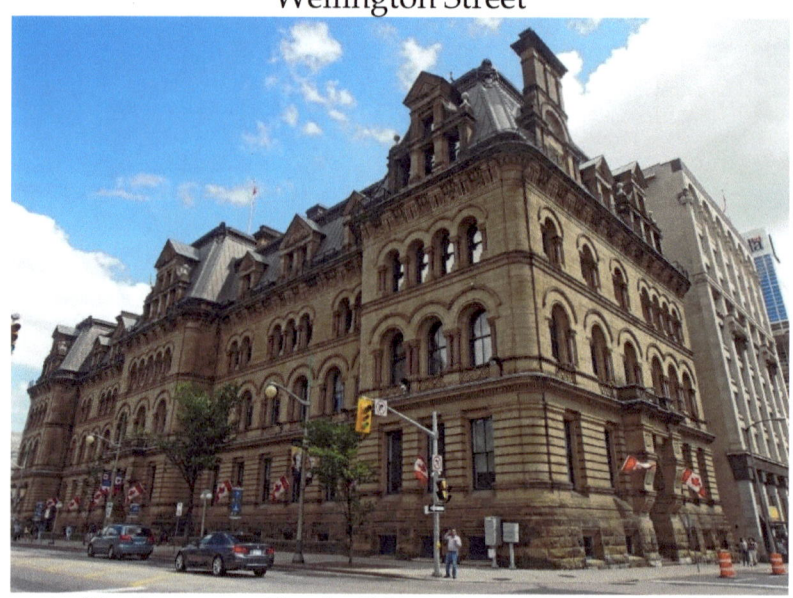

Langevin Block - is an office building facing Parliament Hill. As the home of the Privy Council Office and Office of the Prime Minister, it is the working headquarters of the executive branch of the Canadian government. The building is named after a Father of Confederation and cabinet minister Hector Langevin. Built of sandstone from a New Brunswick quarry between 1884 and 1889 - Second Empire style - Mansard roof, dormers, grotesque sculptures (fantastic or mythical figures used for decorative purposes)

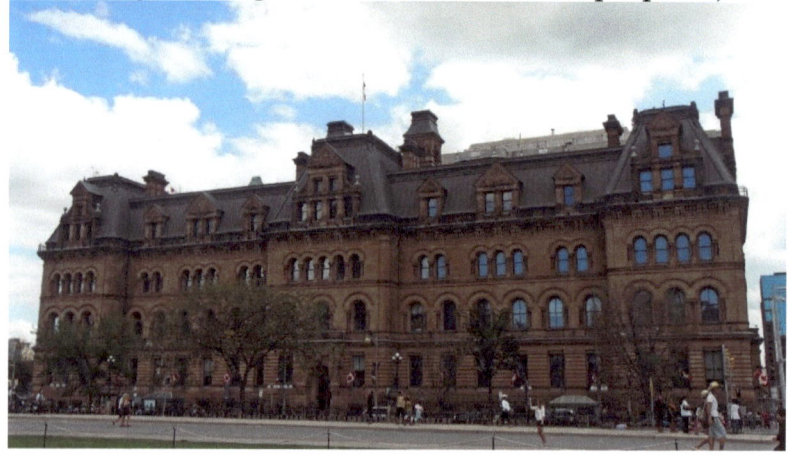

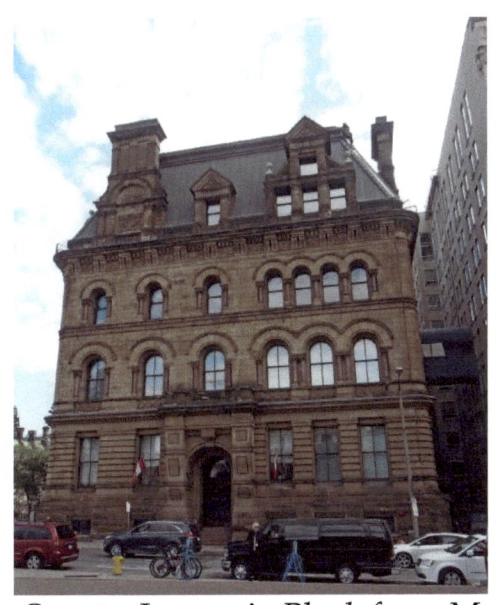

80 Wellington Street – Langevin Block from Metcalfe Street –
Office of the Prime Minister

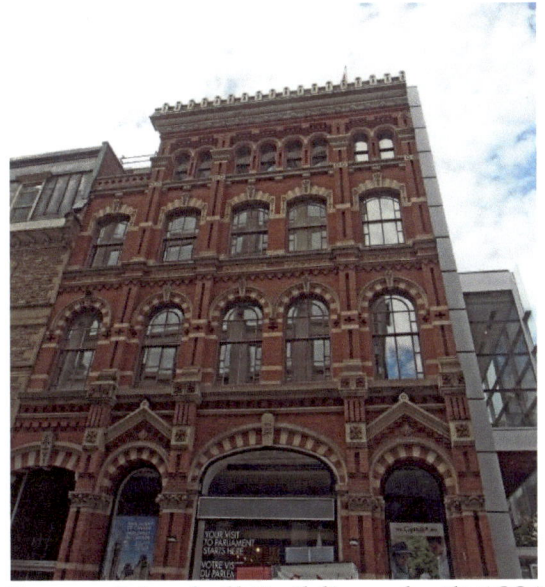

14 Metcalfe Street - Marshall Building - built 1881-1882 – now
operates as a Visitor Information centre – dichromatic
brickwork, pilasters, Corinthian capitals, keystones,
bevelled dentil moulding

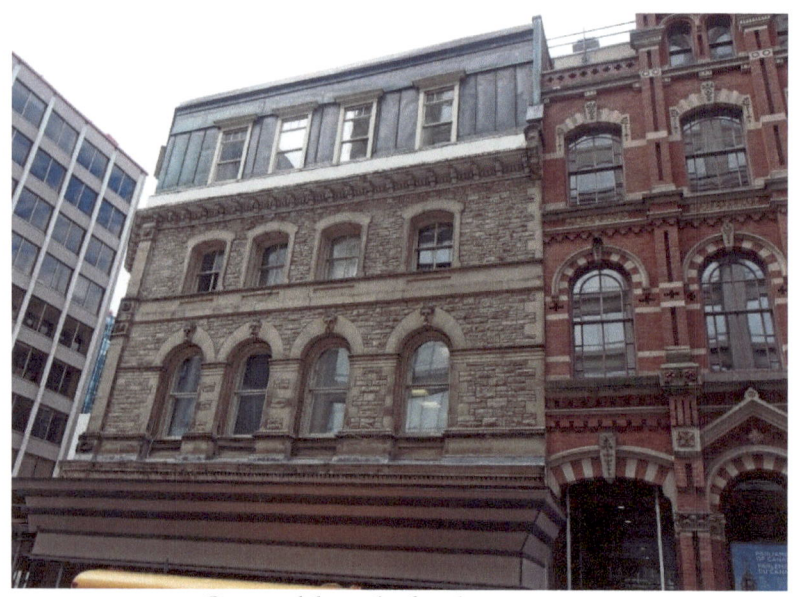

Carved heads for keystones

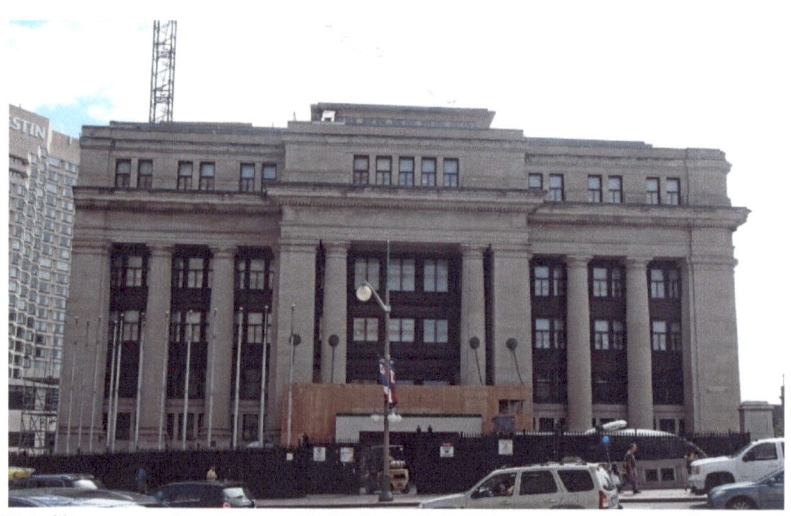

Wellington Street and Colonel By Drive - One of North America's first monumental railway stations, Grand Trunk Railway Union Station opened in 1912 and served passengers until 1966.

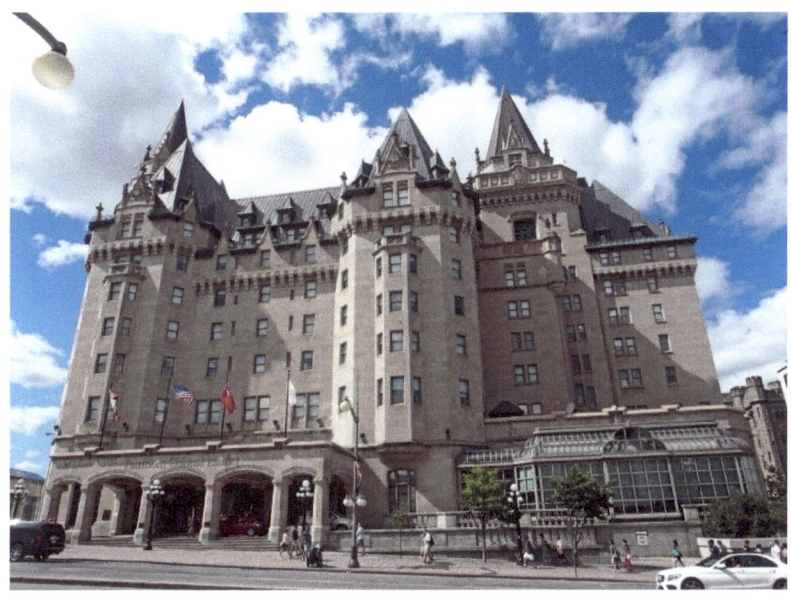

1 Rideau Street - Fairmont Chateau Laurier, one of Canada's landmark railway hotels, built in the Canadian Chateau style

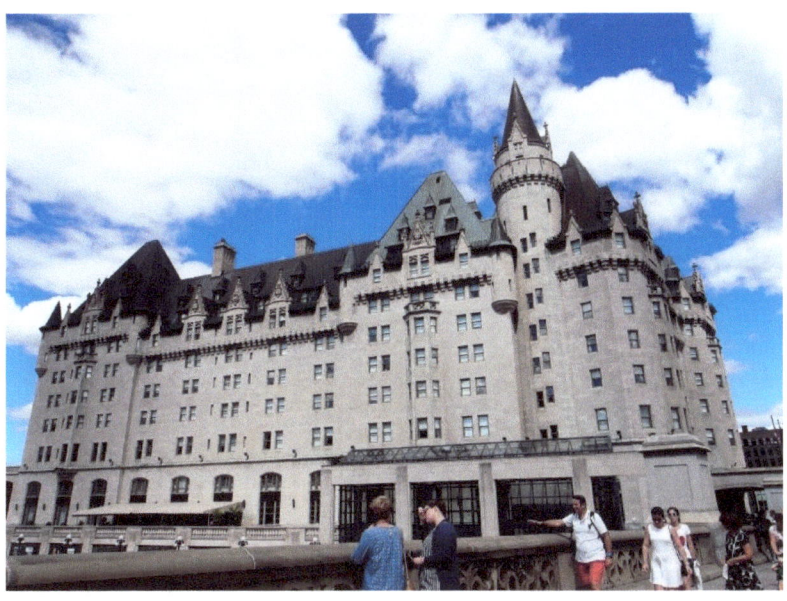

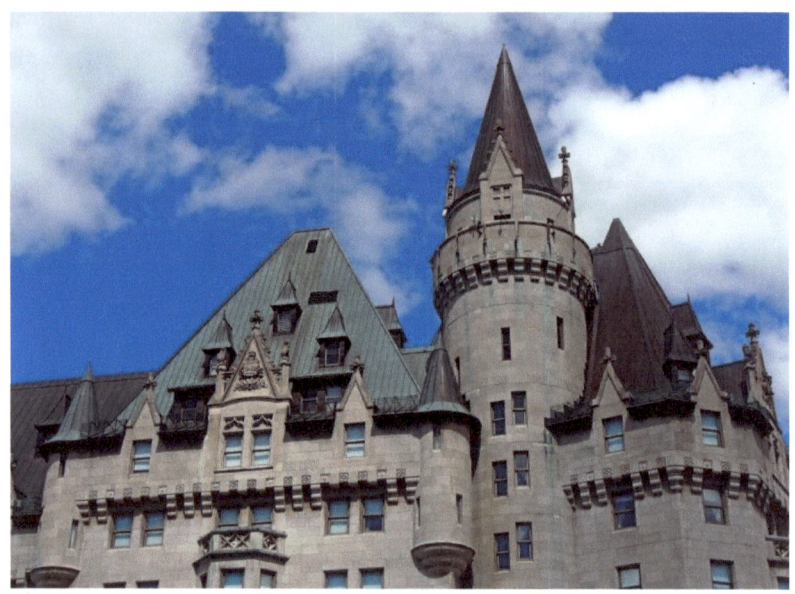

Machiolated tower, tall gabled wall dormers, fractables (irregular, not smooth, curves), corbelled projecting upper floors, battlementing, and steep metal-clad Mansard roof

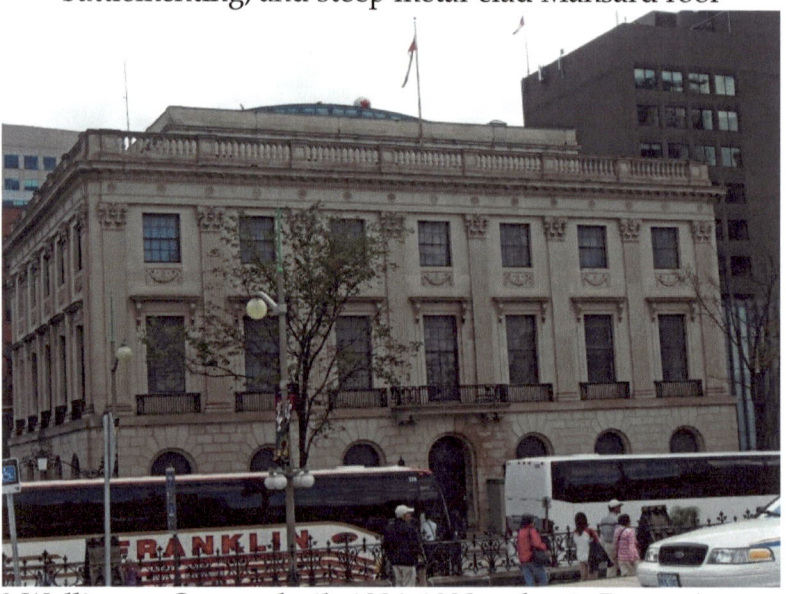

100 Wellington Street – built 1931-1932 – classic Beaux Arts style and finished in limestone - parapet surrounded by spindle railing, pilasters, window hoods, circular decorations

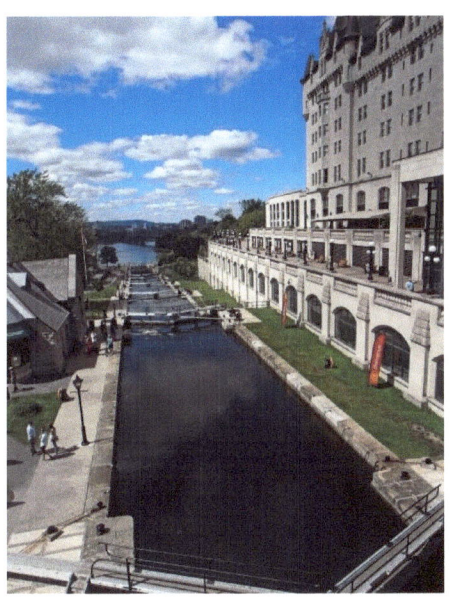

Rideau Canal

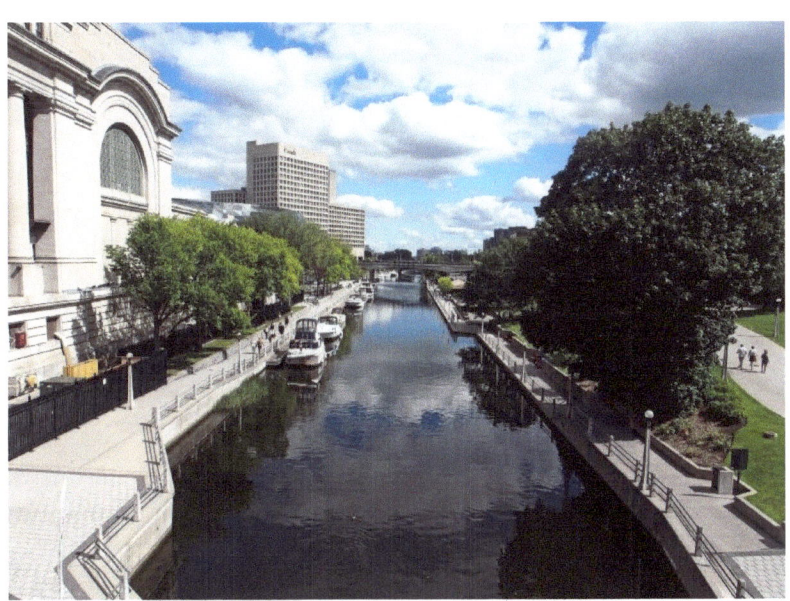

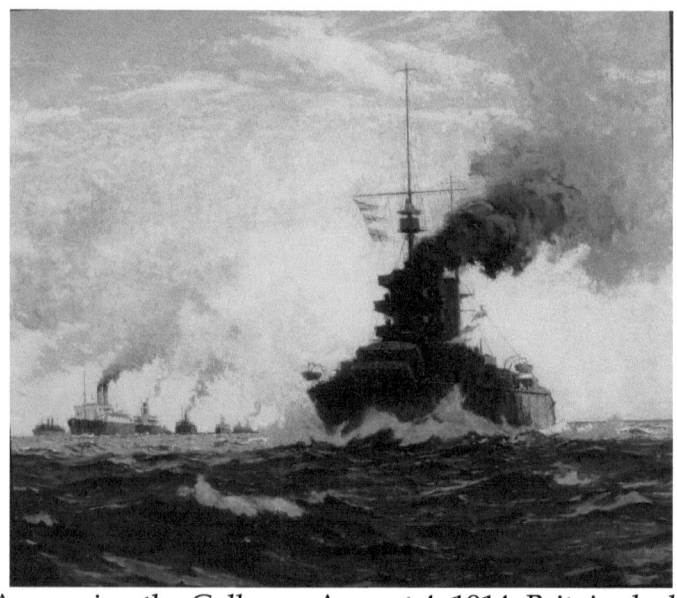

Answering the Call – on August 4, 1914, Britain declared war on Germany. As a British Dominion, Canada was also at war. During August and September, newly gathered Canadian recruits were given basic training at a hastily built camp at Valcartier, Quebec. Troop ships transported the first wave of 32,000 Canadian troops and 500 Newfoundland troops to Britain. At that time, no one knew the horrors that twentieth century industrialized warfare would bring over the next four years.

The First World War was one of the most far-reaching and traumatic events in Canadian history. Most of the Canadians who served in the war were not professional soldiers or battlefield nurses: they were young men and women from cities, towns and farms.

Canadians on the Home Front made important contributions to the war effort by purchasing Victory Bonds, loaning money to their own government to finance the war.

In May 1915, after a friend was killed during the Second Battle of Ypres, John McCrae wrote the poem *In Flanders' Fields*. Today Canadians wear the bright red poppy to remember and honor the men and women who died in war. Canada adopted the poppy as its official symbol of remembrance in 1921.

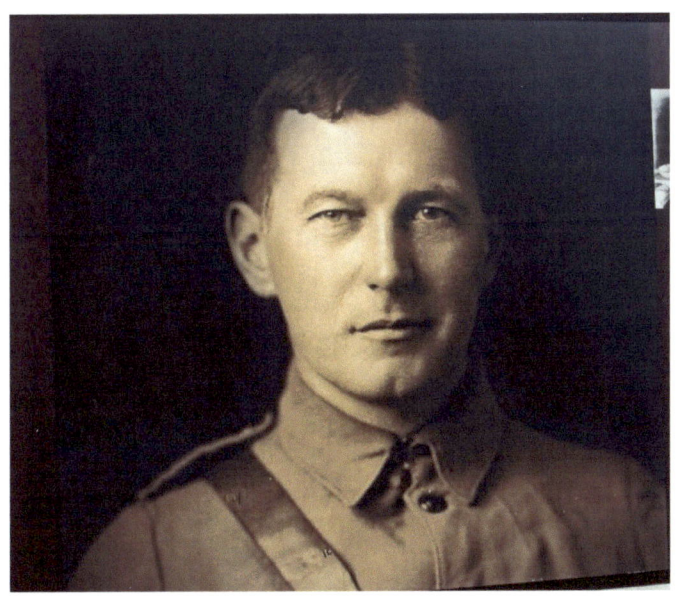

Lieutenant Colonel John McCrae - a physician and trained soldier dedicated to treating war casualties. John McCrae was among the dead, dying of pneumonia on January 28, 1918.

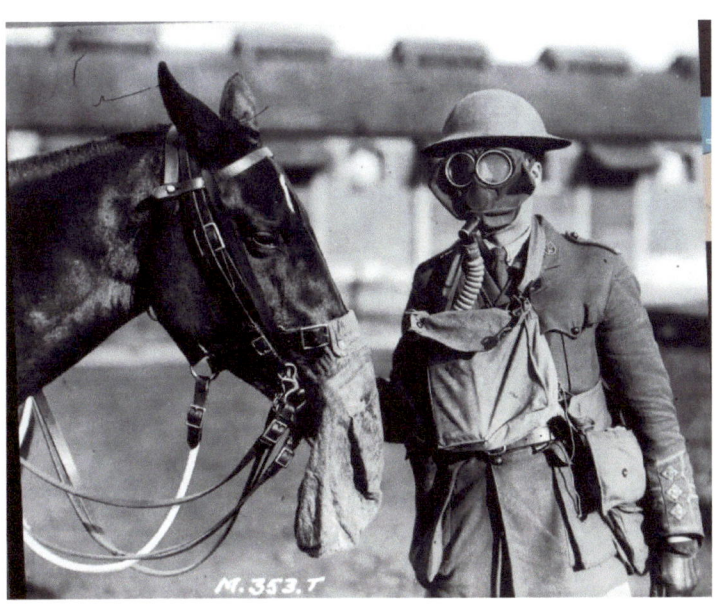

At the Front – Canadian soldiers first arrived in France in large numbers in early 1915. At the Second Battle of Ypres in April 1915, the Canadian Division fought courageously to stop the Germans from capturing the small town of Ypres in Flanders, Belgium.

Outnumbered, the Canadians fought through poison gas to stall the enemy advance, at the cost of almost 6,000 men killed, wounded or taken prisoner. As a result, they earned the reputation of being among the British Empire's best troops.

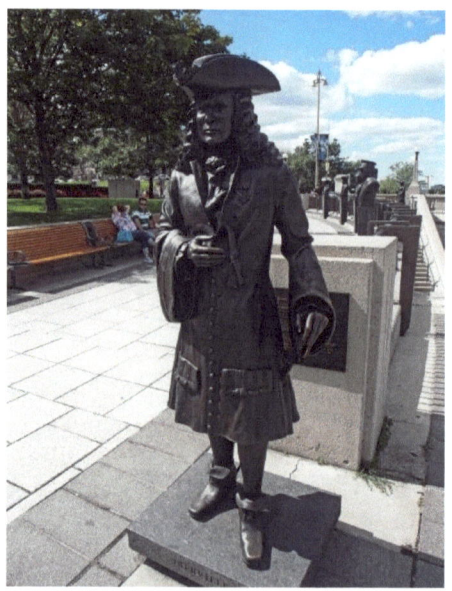

Pierre Le Moyne d'Iberville (1661-1706) was a great commander who fought the English boldly. In 1697 when three English vessels attacked his ship, *the Pelican*, in Hudson Bay, he sank one, boarded another, and then captured their outpost at York Fort.

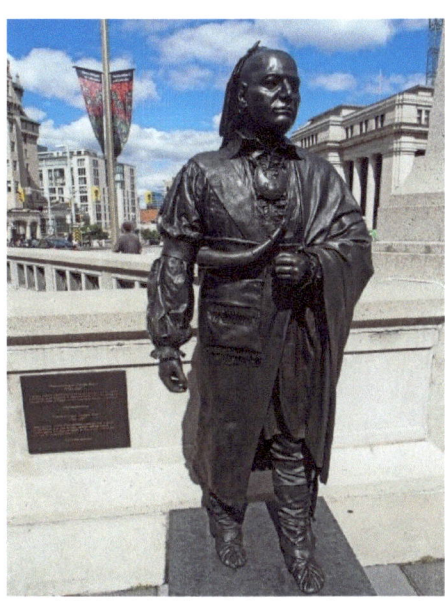

Chief Joseph Brant (1742-1807) – Mohawk warrior and statesman, and principal war chief of the Six Nations, he led his people in support of the British during the American Revolution. After the war, he brought his people to Canada to settle near what is now Brantford.

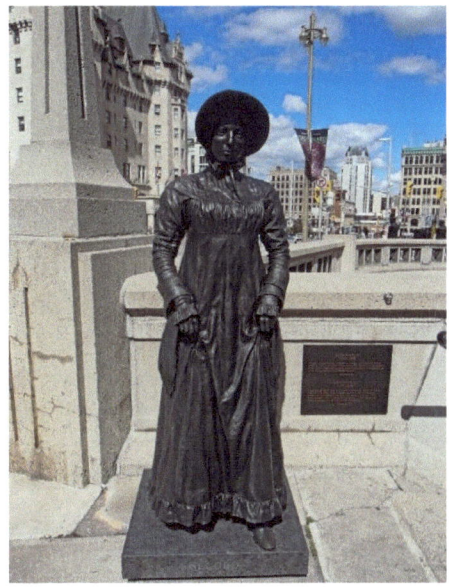

Laura Secord warned the British that the Americans were coming.

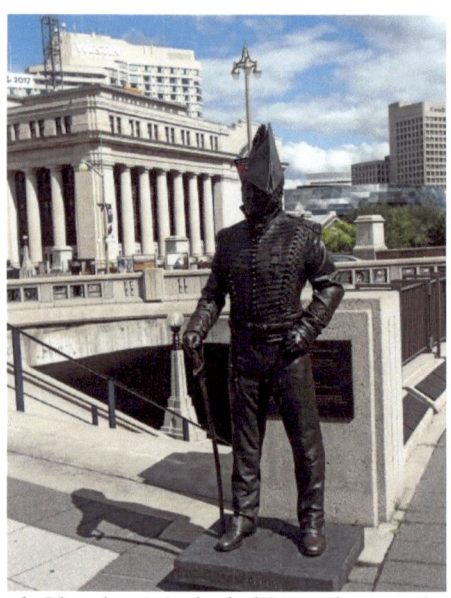

Lieutenant Colonel Charles Michel d'Irumberry de Salaberry was a skillful professional soldier who formed the celebrated Voltigeurs Canadiens. In 1813, he outwitted and defeated a vastly superior American force at the Battle of Chateauguay, helping to save Lower Canada from invasion during the War of 1812.

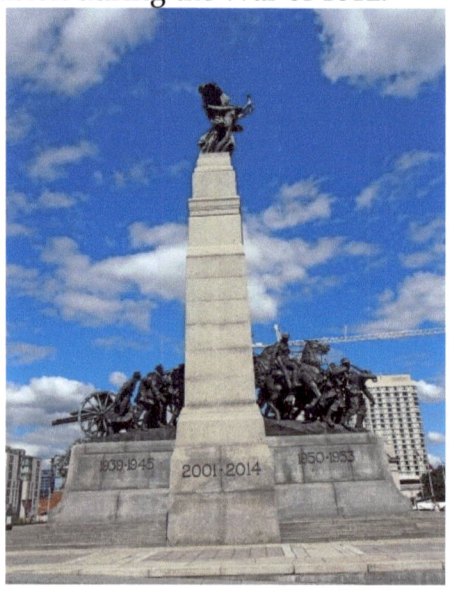

Confederation Square and the National War Memorial

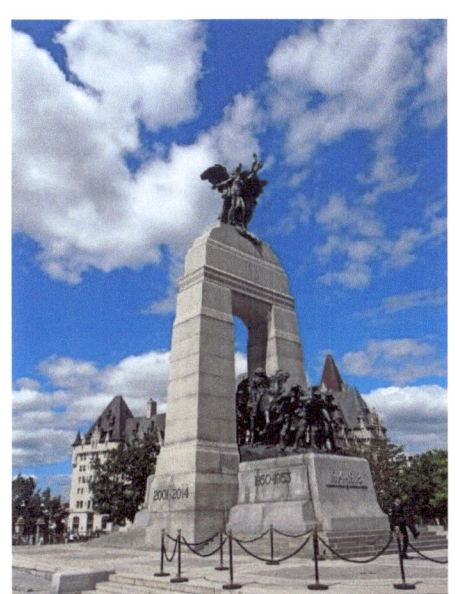

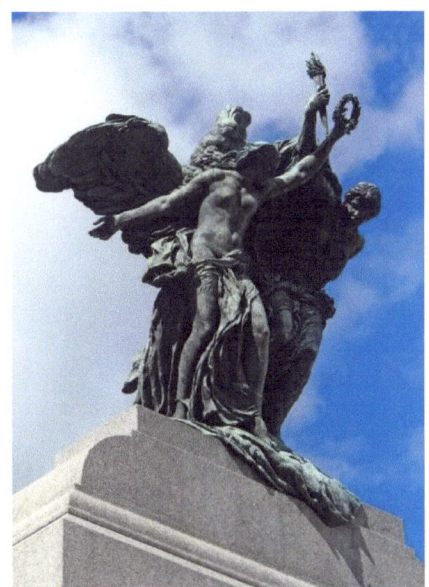

Confederation Square and the National War Memorial titled
The Response – the figures represent all of the forces engaged in
the First World War; the figures of Peace holding a laurel
wreath, and Liberty holding a torch adorn the top of the
monument's arch

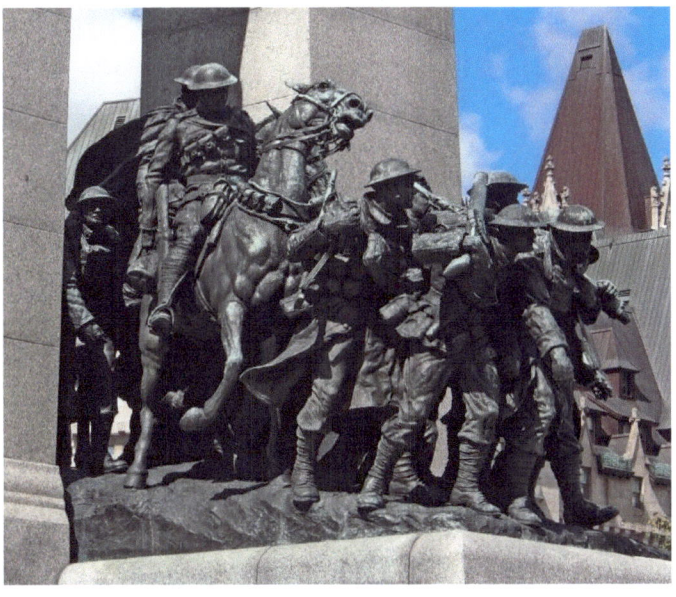

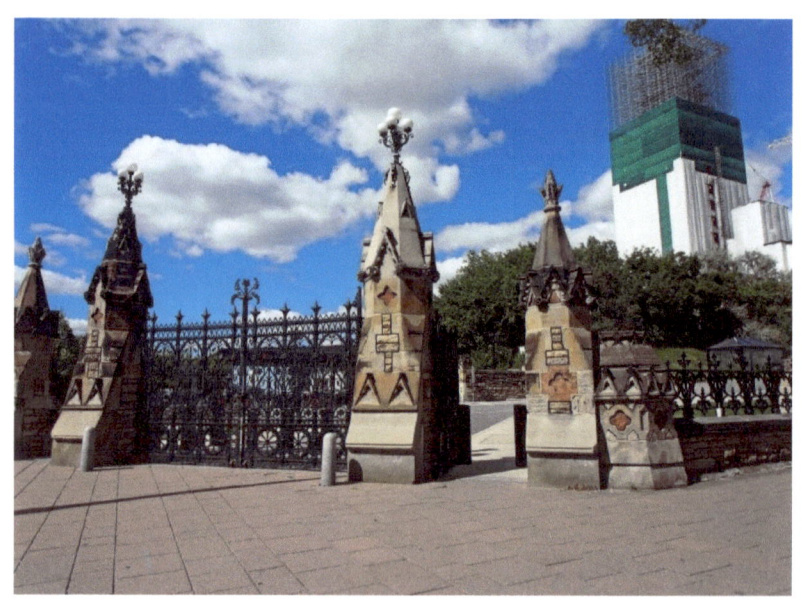

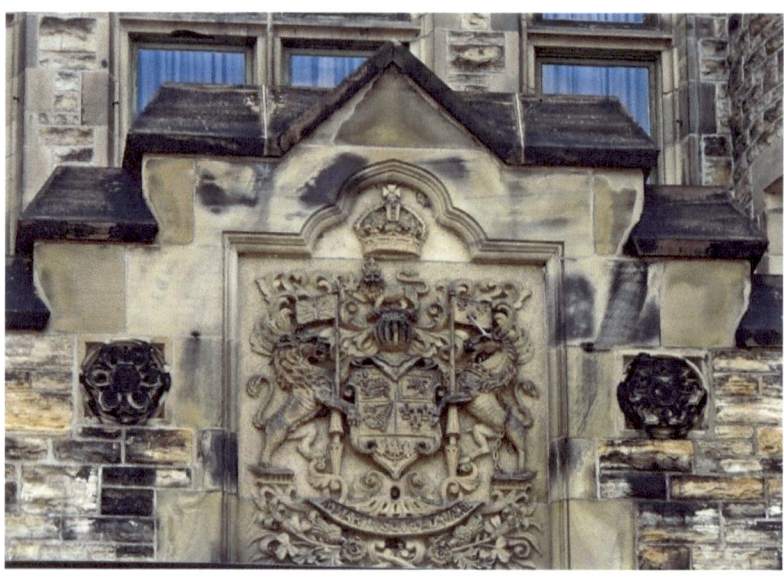

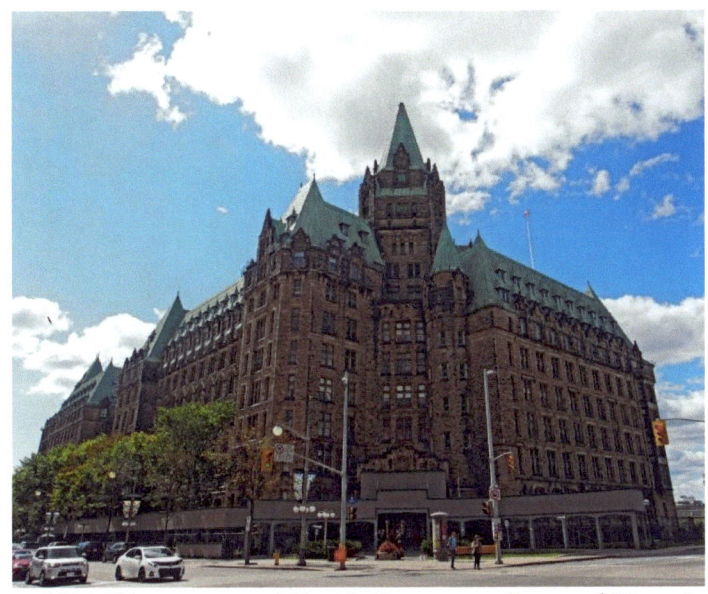

Corner of Wellington and Bank Streets – Second Empire style,
Mansard roof

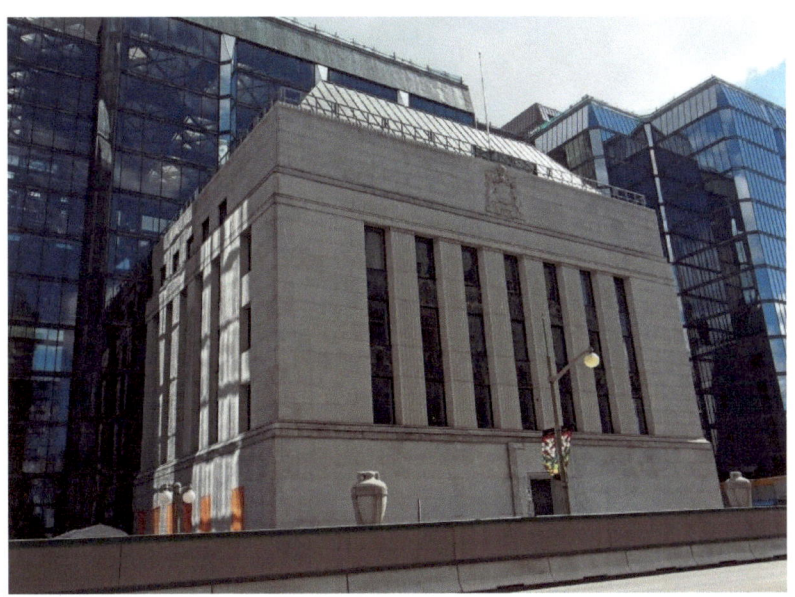

234 Wellington Street - Bank of Canada – completed in 1938 –
five-storey Neo-Classical building; the modern glass
courtyard and towers behind were completed in 1979

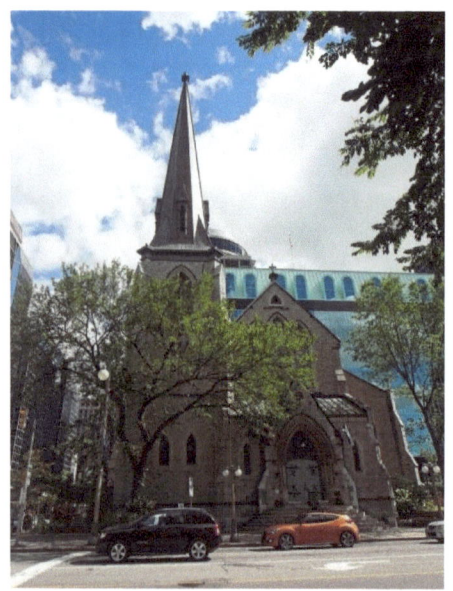

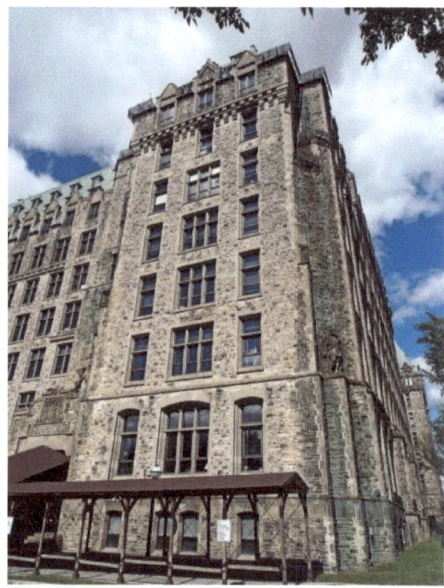

82 Kent Street - St. Andrew's
Presbyterian Church – 1872
Gothic, lancet windows, buttresses

294 Wellington Street
Justice Building

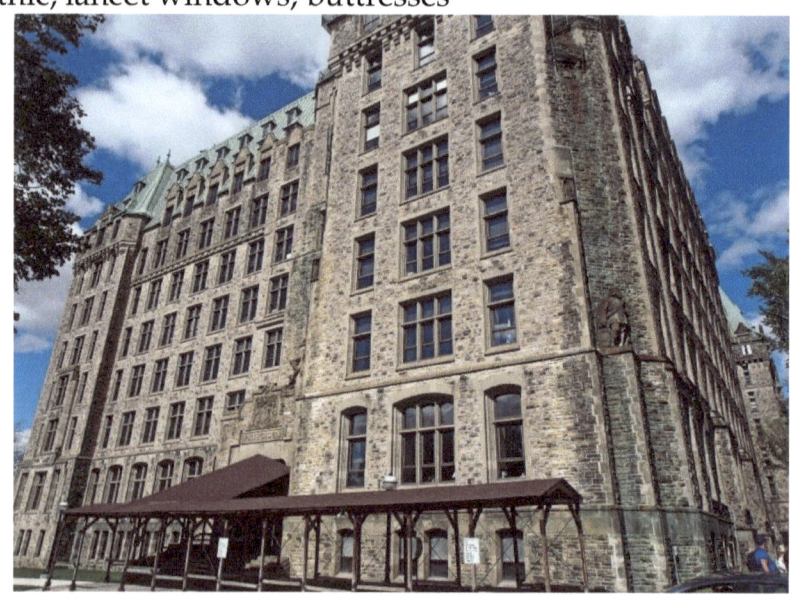

Justice Building – built 1935-1938 – Chateau style – 9 storeys

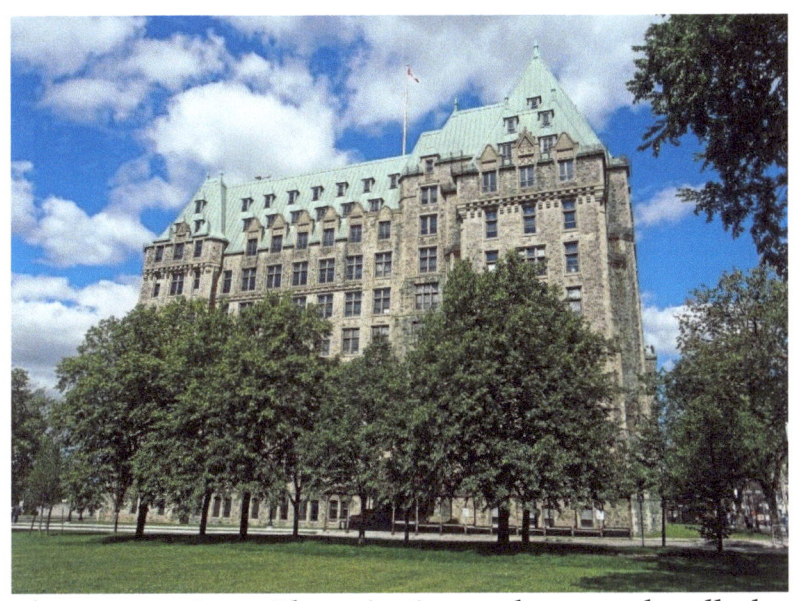

Sandstone exterior with projecting and recessed wall planes; high, steep copper roof; dormers, turrets, tall windows, pavilions and towers give a strong vertical emphasis

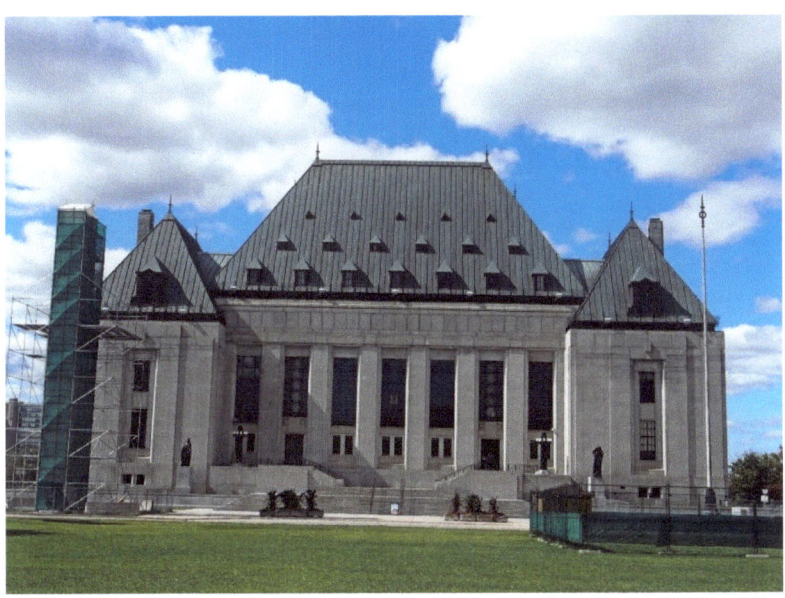

301 Wellington Street - Supreme Court of Canada – Art Deco style with a Chateauesque roof – built between 1939 and 1945

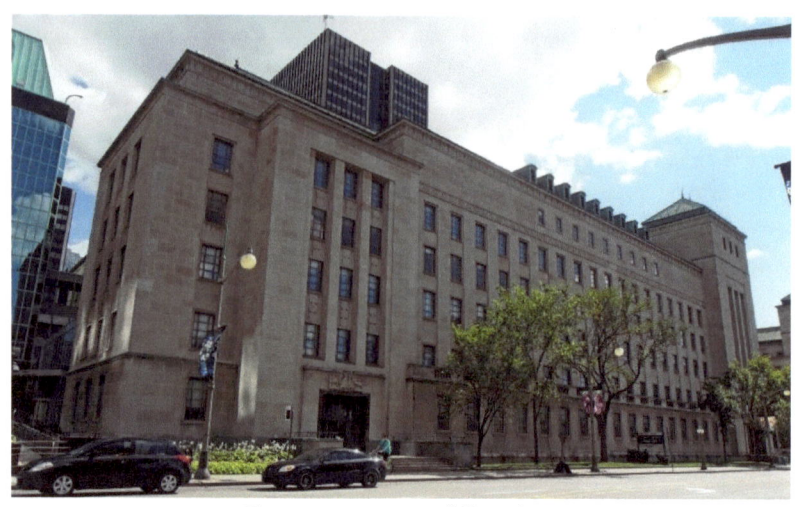

Department of Justice

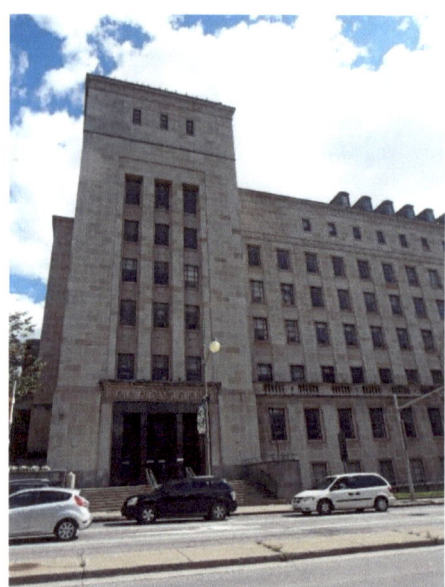

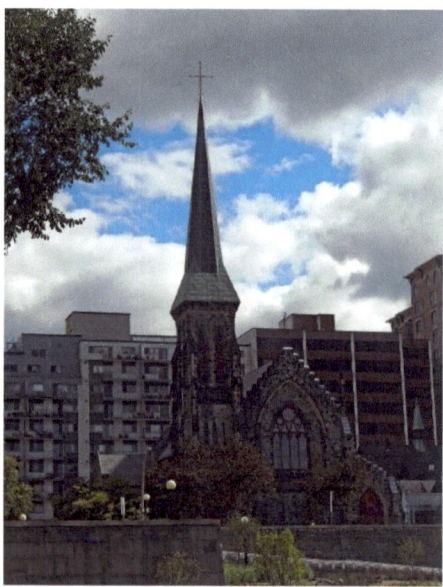

344 Wellington Street – 1955
West Memorial Building
Art Deco style

Gothic church building

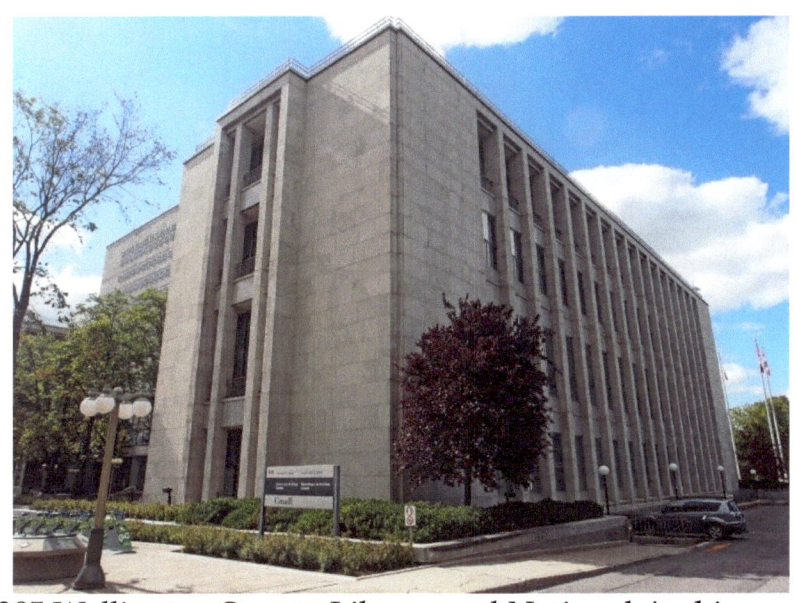

395 Wellington Street - Library and National Archives of Canada

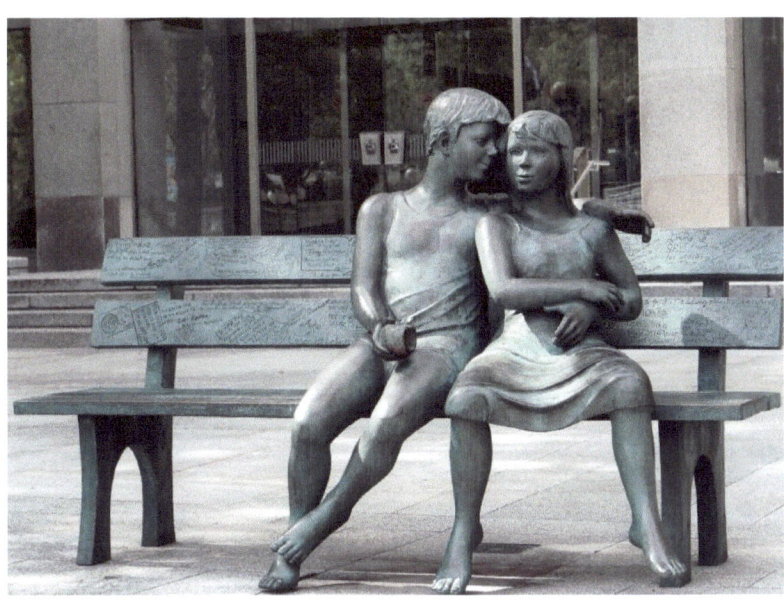

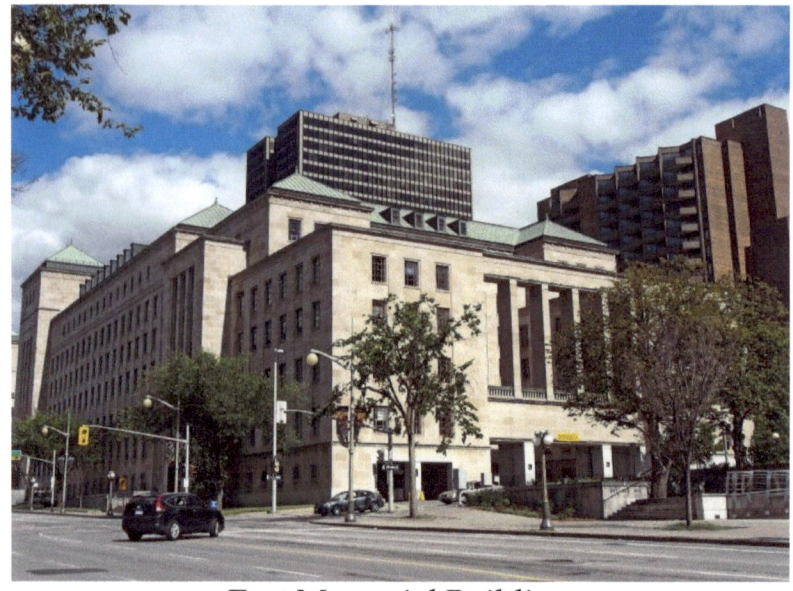

East Memorial Building

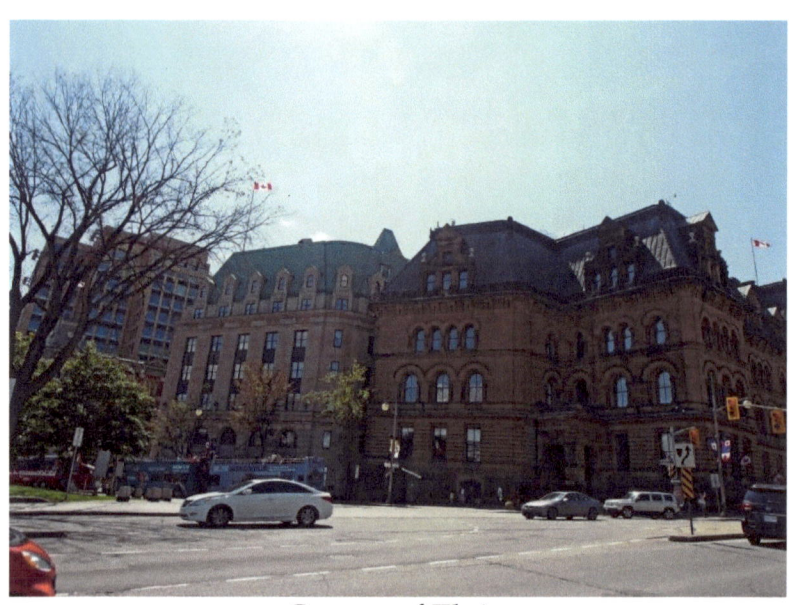

Corner of Elgin

Architectural Terms

Battlement: A design for a parapet that has alternating solid parts and openings, originally used for defense, but later used as a decorative motif. Example: Fairmont Chateau Laurier, Page 14	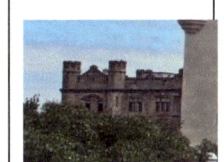
Buttress: a masonry structure built against or projecting from a wall which serves to support or reinforce the wall. In Canadian architecture, they are sometimes used for decoration. Example: Library of Parliament, Page 23	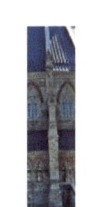
Capital: The uppermost finish or decoration on a column. A Corinthian column is characterized by a rounded capital decorated with acanthus leaves and a square abacus (the uppermost portion of a capital directly below the entablature) on tall slender columns. Example: 14 Metcalfe Street, Page 43	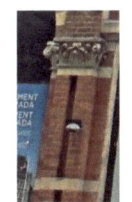
Corbel: Corbelling is the original method of making arches a series of stones or bricks that protrude beyond the lower level to finally cover the arch. Corbels are used to support cornices, turrets, brackets, ribs and oriel windows. A corbel is also a stone or piece of wood that supports a super incumbent weight. Example: Fairmont Chateau Laurier, Page 46	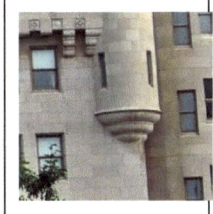

Dentil Moulding: an even series of rectangles used as ornamental decoration in cornices. Example: 14 Metcalfe Street, Page 43	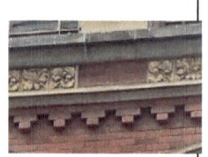
Dichromatic brickwork: the use of two colours of brick, tile or slate to decorate a façade. Example: 14 Metcalfe Street, Page 43	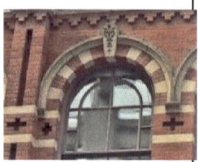
Dome: Any roof structure that is curved and spans a circular base. Example: Library of Parliament, Page 23	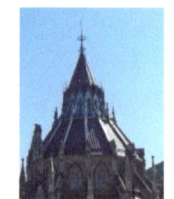
Dormer: (French for "sleep") a gable end window that pierces through the plane of a sloping roof surface to create usable space in the top floor or attic of a building by adding headroom. Example: 80 Wellington Street, Page 42	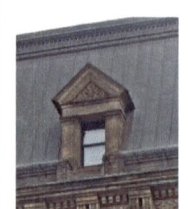
Gable: the triangular portion of a wall between the edges of a sloping roof. Example: Wellington Street, Page 58	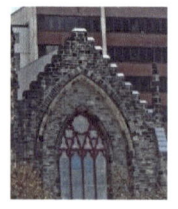

Iron Cresting: A decorative ornament along the top of a roof. Iron cresting was popular in the Baroque era and also in Italianate, Victorian, Second Empire and Queen Anne styles of architecture. Example: East Block, Page 11	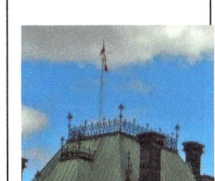
Keystone is the central stone that locks all the stones into position, allowing the arch to bear weight. A keystone is often enlarged and embellished. Example: Wellington Street, Page 44	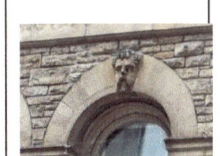
Lancet Window: a tall, narrow window with a pointed arch at its top. Example: 82 Kent Street, Page 56	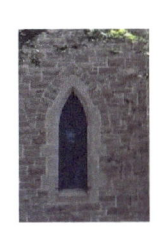
Machicolation: On castles and fortifications in the middle ages, parapets were often extended out on corbels so that they projected beyond the wall and left an opening through which missiles could be launched at advancing assailants. Later this design was used as a decorative accent on towers. Example: Fairmont Chateau Laurier, Page 46	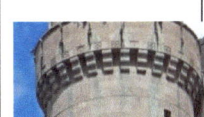

Mansard Roof: This style was popularized by Francois Mansart (1598-1666), an accomplished architect of the French Baroque period and especially fashionable during the Second French Empire (1852-1870). This roof is almost flat on the top section, with two slopes on each of its sides with the lower slope at a steeper angle than the upper and having dormer windows. Example: Langevin Block, Page 42	
Parapet: low wall around the edge of a roof. Example: 100 Wellington Street, Page 46	
Pilaster: a slightly projecting column built into or applied to the face of a wall for additional structural support. Example: 100 Wellington Street, Page 46	
Turret: a small tower that projects from the wall of a building. Example: Fairmont Chateau Laurier, Page 46	
Window Hood: A **hood** is the piece found above window openings, usually of an ornate design, and covers the top third of the opening. Hoods are commonly placed above arched or curved openings on both windows and doors. Example: 100 Wellington Street, Page 46	

Building Styles

Art Deco, 1910-1940 - The Art Deco Style was developed for the French luxury market after World War I. Art Deco left its mark on everything from lamps and foot stools to purses and hair combs. The style was adopted in Ontario by wealthy and very fashionable patrons who wanted Art Deco detailing to make their buildings look lavish and exotic. Example: 344 Wellington Street, Page 58	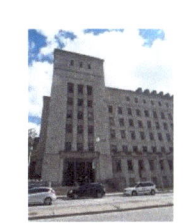
Beaux Arts: Promoters of this style sought to express the classical principles on a grand and imposing scale. Many of the Beaux Arts buildings were banks, post offices, and railway stations. The Ontario Beaux Arts style is eclectic mixing elements of Classical, Renaissance and Baroque. Often the designs have a temple-like façade, porticos with pediments, balustrades, and capitals in many styles. Example: 100 Wellington Street, Page 46	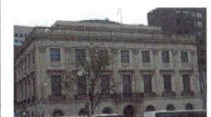

Château (1880 - 1930)**:** **T**he Château Style is a grand adaptation of the sixteenth-century French chateaux of the Loire Valley. The fortified castles of medieval France were translated in Ontario into asymmetrical, irregular and equally elegant hotels, convents, and imposing private houses for the wealthy. The bases of this style are steeply pitched roofs with plenty of dormers, turrets, gables, conical towers, lunettes, and iron cresting. Ornamentation is lavish with intricate string courses, corbel tables, finials and crockets. The walls are generally finished stone or stucco and the roofs, especially on commercial buildings, are often copper left to develop a patina of soft green. Example: 1 Rideau Street, Page 45	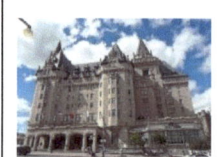
Gothic Revival, 1830-1890 – These decorative buildings have sharply-pitched gables with highly detailed verge boards, pointed-arch window openings, and dichromatic brickwork. It is a common style in Ontario. Example: Parliament Buildings, Page 12	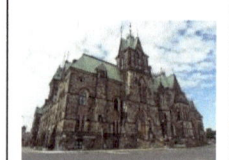
Second Empire, 1860-1880 – The mansard roof is the most noteworthy feature of this style and is evidence of the French origins. Projecting central towers and one or two-storey bays can also be present. Example: Langevin Block, Page 42	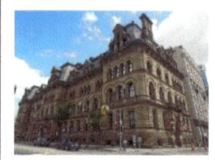

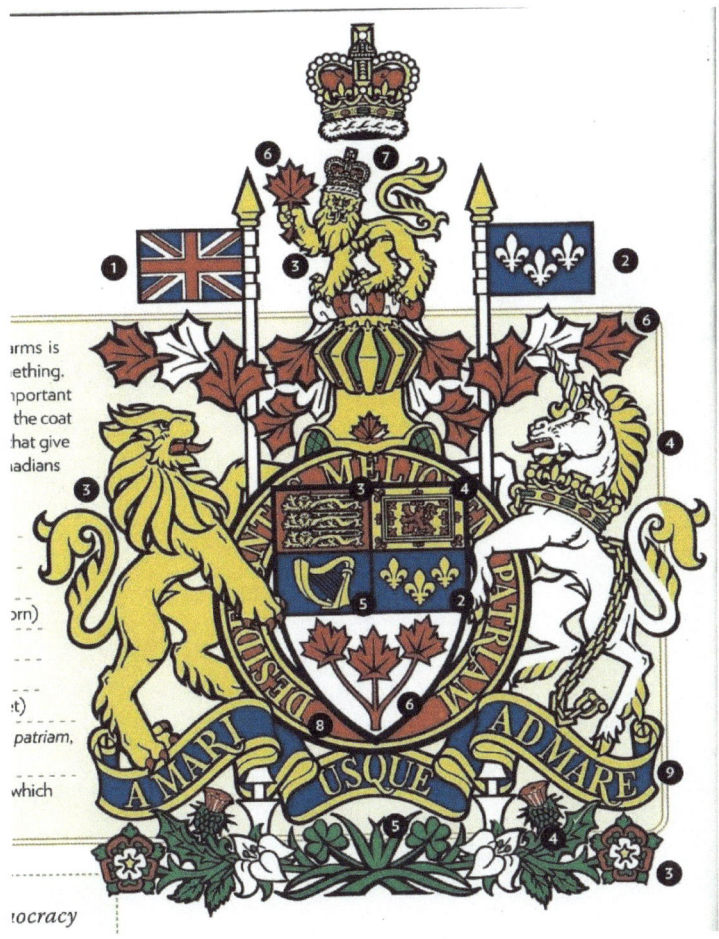

Canadian Coat of Arms

1 the flag of the United Kingdom
2 the royal flag of France (fleur-de-lis)
3 symbols of England (golden lions, roses)
4 symbols of Scotland (red lion, thistles, unicorn)
5 symbols of Ireland (harp, shamrocks)
6 Canadian symbols (maple leaves)
7 symbols of monarchy (crowns, royal helmet)
8 the words in Latin *desiderantes meliorem patriam* which means *they desire a better country*
9 the words in Latin *a mari usque ad mare* which means *from sea to sea*

www.ingramcontent.com/pod-product-compliance
Lightning Source LLC
Chambersburg PA
CBHW040842180526
45159CB00001B/284